Living Largely

Neil P. Smith

Kingdom Kaught Publishing LLC
Denton Maryland

This book was printed in the United States of America.

Copyright © 2011 by Neil P. Smith

All rights reserved. No part of this book may be reproduced or transmitted in any form or by any means without written permission of the author.

Unless otherwise indicated, all Scripture quotations are taken from the NEW KING JAMES VERSION, copyright © 1979, 1980, 1982 by Thomas Nelson, Inc. Publishers and from THE MESSAGE copyright © 1993, 1994, 1995, 1996, 2000, 2001, 2002 used by permission of NavPress Publishing Group. Scripture quotations noted NIV aare from the HOLY BIBLE: NEW INTERNATIONAL VERSION® Copyright © 1973, 1978, 1984 by International Bibles Society, used by permission of Zondervan Publishing House. All rights reserved.

Copyediting by Antonio Palmer, antonio.palmer@ymail.com

Cover Design by Agape Adverstisement, Inc.

Cover image by Michael Wilde Photography, www.mbwilde.com, mikebwilde@gmail.com

ISBN: 978-0-9824550-3-6
Library of Congress Control Number: 2011928924

Dedication

I would like to dedicate this book to my Lord and Savior Jesus Christ who has loved me and taught me to live largely. And to my lovely wife and best friend, Julie, who has stood with me, and encouraged me along the way. To my daughters, Kaitlin and Madison, who inspire me to live and make me stretch so that they can enjoy a large life and a greater future. To my mother, Nina J. Smith, and my sister, Susan, who taught me what true believers look like. And to my grandmother, Edna Miller whose mantle I continue to carry. To my pastors and mentors, Bishop Michael and Tena Sloan, who saw something in me that I couldn't see in myself; who kept speaking into me until this book came out of me. And finally, to my Aunt and Uncle, Deborah and John Youngblood, who not only encouraged me, but opened their lives and home to me at the most challenging time in my life.

Acknowledgements

I would like to thank the many friends and encouragers who have helped me give birth to this baby. Throughout the years they have encouraged me, chided me, pushed me, and a couple of times almost shoved me to get out of my comfort zone and to write. Thanks to each of you, I love you more than there is room to write!

Special thanks to Dorris Wisner, who took on the task of editing my project as I typed, you are the best! Thanks and blessings to Pastor Ernest E. Brown, Dr. Peggy Scarborough, Janet Betts, my Oasis World Outreach Family, Pastor Rich Jividen, Rev. Jesse Wilson, and the many family members and friends that read Neil's Notes week after week and year after year and still say, "You should write a book!"

I did and here it is…Let's Live Large Together!

Foreword

When I was asked by Neil to be a part of the forward of this book, I immediately thought of our great friendship and the honor I had been given! Just by its title "Living Largely" speaks volumes of the passion and purpose of its author. I know him well! I also was taken back to an encounter I had with God in 1998 while at my present pastorate.

As a youngster growing up in Arkansas and then at the age of eleven moving to a small town in Florida, I had always had a dream of one day seeing the Grand Canyon! Having only seen pictures or reading about it, it seemed worlds away. As I grew older and began to follow God's plan for my life, the opportunity came while on a staff trip to see the Canyon. I will never forget that day!

The moment we rounded a curve and I saw the sight, my breath was literally taken away! I was speechless...this boy from Arkansas was finally here. Getting out of the car on that cold February day, wind blowing, I walked to its rim. My feet were half on and half off the edge and I can only describe my experience as a "God Encounter".

I could hear those who were traveling with me shouting "Come back, you are too close to the edge, you may fall!" But at that moment in time, I had no fear. God was speaking to me and this is what I heard Him say, "Jump into My bigness!" It was at that point that I understood why He had brought me to this place and even as a young boy put this desire in my spiritual DNA! Needless to say, my life has never been the same.

I believe this is exactly what this book is all about. The bigness of God for your life will challenge you to go beyond your limits and tap into your spiritual DNA. Move into the big things of God for your life!

If Neil Smith was ever created to do anything besides being a great preacher and pastor, he was created to write. I believe it is a God-thing that his first book is "Living Largely." This book is a part of his spiritual DNA. As you read it, I believe your life will be challenged to move beyond its present limits and move to a place of living largely!

Michael E. Sloan
Bishop & Senior Pastor, Oasis World Outreach
Zephyrhills, FL

Endorsements

There are individuals that have gone through life merely in existence without having ever lived. They sit on the sidelines of life cheering for others to do something spectacular, and fail to recognize that God has a mind-blowing plan for their life as well. Your past is a memory; your present is an opportunity; and your future is your destiny. You can do nothing about then, but you can do everything about now! In this dynamic revelation, Living Largely, Neil reveals life changing truths that will encourage readers to disregard mediocrity, and embrace the totality of the life that God has intended for them to live. This book will not only inspire you, but it will challenge you to become more than you are presently. Don't wait the time is now to begin your journey of "Living Largely".

C.D. Nesbitt
Senior Leader, Glory Center International
Champaign, IL

What an exciting book! Neil Smith has given us a clear roadmap for living the abundant life. God sent every one of us into the world with an exciting plan and purpose that no one else can fulfill. The principles in this book will help you get excited about fulfilling your ordained destiny.

For years it has been evident that Neil has a mandate to write to the body of Christ. Many of us have prayed for this day that he would put into print the greatness that God has deposited in him. I highly recommend this book and pray that God will bless you as you begin to live largely.

Dr. Peggy Scarborough
Author, *Healing Through Spiritual Warfare,*
Conference Speaker
Myrtle Beach, SC

I am fortunate to know Neil Smith for many years. I think of him as a part of my spiritual family. It is apparent to me that he hears things in the realm of the Holy Spirit that is often overlooked in the Kingdom of God. His words speak powerfully of a person who has found the Secret of the Stairs, into the Holy Place of the Lord. I am often amazed at his clarity of truth, and the insight as well as perspective that he speaks from. I believe he HEARS from the Lord. He has ears that HEAR what the Holy Spirit is saying to the Church today. It is my pleasure to be connected with him in the Family of God!

REPUTATION CHANGES – CHARACTER GROWS – INTEGRITY LEADS

THINK right--TALK right--WALK right--It's that SIMPLE!

Ernest E. Brown, Th. D., Pastor
The Christian Center
Arab, Alabama
www.thechristiancenter.us

Table of Contents

Introduction 1

Chapter 1 - Happy Meals or Super Sized? 3

Chapter 2 - Learning to Live Largely *(Isaiah 54:1)* 7

Chapter 3 - S. E. E. *(Isaiah 54:2)* 17

Chapter 4 - Living Life like a Rubber Band *(Isaiah 54:2)* 25

Chapter 5 - Change the Label *(Isaiah 54:4)* 31

Chapter 6 - Got a Minute? *(Isaiah 54:6-10)* 37

Chapter 7 - Winner from Within *(Isaiah 54:11-17)* 43

Chapter 8 - Connect the Dots 49

Chapter 9 - Living Now in the Now 69

Chapter 10 - Living Larger than Ourselves *(Isaiah 60:1-2)* ... 83

Chapter 11 - Going to the Next Level *(1 Kings 19:19-21)* 91

Chapter 12 - Become What You Believe! *(Matthews 9:27-31)* 99

Conclusion 113

Citations 115

About the Author

Introduction

When God created you, he did so with the finished product in mind. In Genesis 2 we read where God says, "Let us make man in our image and in our likeness." The prophet Isaiah said that God has graven our image in the palm of His hand. You have your heavenly Father's DNA, you look just like Him, and when He wants to remind Himself of you, He looks into His hand and sees your individual design.

We live in an image conscious world; product labels, brand names, specific types of makeup, designer clothing, all of these things are used to create a certain image. The Body of Christ has used similar means to create or recreate their image. We have created "Christian Branding" and "Designer Labels" to make ourselves known and to feel comfortable in the world. Many Christians are living frustrated lives, depressed and discouraged, unable to meet the standards that others have observed and that they themselves have self-imposed.

The Bible clearly declares that when God created us, He made us to look like Him and to reflect His image; we are the visible means by which others come to see and know Christ. The creation account in Genesis says that whenever God created anything, He would observe it and then say, "It is good!"

When God created you to look and act like Him, when He made you He placed in you certain qualities and personality traits that are assigned specifically to you. These personality traits make up your character, your Spiritual DNA; they make you who and what you are, and as you nurture and develop them, God observes them and says..."It is good!"

As I read the scriptures I am convinced that God not only created us to look like Him, but to act like Him, and to live like Him. God's command to the first man was to be fruitful, to multiply, and to have dominion in the earth. That commandment hasn't changed. God continues to call us to have dominion, to tread down the opposition, to subdue our enemies, and to cause opposing forces to be subject to the Christ that dwells within us. In essence, we are called to live largely!

This is a book about living largely; about experiencing off-the-chart life and living life to the fullest. It's about seeing God and yourself in a different manner. It's about getting big on the inside...it's time for you to be Living Largely!

Chapter 1

Happy Meals or Super Sized?

As a boy growing up the choices were limited when it came to what size burgers and fries we chose. Hamburgers and fries came in one size for everyone; no one ever gave any thought to anything different. Times have certainly changed. These days you can get a regular hamburger, a quarter-pounder or now even a massive Angus burger and French fries come in three sizes - small, medium, and large.

Recently I was eating at a local McDonald's with my family and some youth from our church. The range of foods was enormous; my daughter had a Happy Meal, a smaller sized meal for younger children. Sitting next to me were some college students and each of these young men had quarter pounders, twenty piece McNuggets, and Super Sized fries. I have to tell you, I was impressed at the amount of food these young men were able to consume. It also inspired me, and created within me a hunger for something more than the usual food, something beyond the grasp of normal.

Jesus came into the world to give us abundant life. Scripture declares that we have already received an abundant entrance into the Kingdom of God, that we have been translated from the kingdom of darkness into the Kingdom of God's Son. In fact, the Bible plainly declares that we as believers have literally changed-- not only our nature, but our address; we have become citizens of heaven. The Apostle Peter declares that we have received a divine nature and exceeding great and precious promises (2 Peter 1:4); the Apostle Paul states that we are already seated in heavenly places in Christ Jesus (Ephesians 2:6), and that all of the promises of God are already ours (2 Corinthians 1:20).

When you read these words and look at how so many believers live you wonder if we're talking about the same thing. Take a quick trip through the New Testament and you find normal, everyday people just like yourself that are serving this mighty God and living extraordinary lives. You read things like, "These are they that have turned the world upside down!"(Acts 17:6) Where are those people in this generation?

God has called us to live largely, to take a risk and reach beyond our limitations. Remember Abram? God came to this simple man in the middle of the desert and gave him a prophetic promise: Get up, Get Out, and Go! Leave your family and friends, leave what is familiar and safe to you and I will make your name great, I will bless you and multiply you, everywhere you go, everywhere you step, I will give it to you. That's large!

Living large is choice, the promise has already been given to us, and it's up to us to walk it out. Your life is like an order of fries: you can be a Happy Meal, just enough to satisfy your hunger, or you can be a Regular fry, you know…normal, just like everyone else. Normal people do what everyone else does, they follow the same path that everyone else is following, do what everyone else is doing. Normal people never make any waves. They simply live in the same mundane mediocre manner that they've always lived.

Happy Meals or Super Sized?

You can get to heaven being normal, your sins are forgiven, you'll make it through the pearly gates, but that's it…you'll just make it.

Let me ask you a question. Do you ever look around and say to yourself, "There's got to be more?"

Do you ever see other family members and friends living abundantly and wonder "Why not me?"

You need to super size your life! We've all seen that super sized order of fries; maybe even attempted to devour the whole thing yourself. Super sized orders are larger than life. It seems like there are more fries than it is possible for one person to eat, and it's a challenge to eat them all. When we lived in Louisville, KY, there was a place called Ginny's Diner. Their claim to fame was a pound and half hamburger, it was massive, four levels of meat. I never finished it, but that was the challenge, to live large enough to give it a try.

What would happen if we decided to super size our lives? What would happen if you determined to live life largely? How would your life change if you made the decision to move from Happy Meal Living to a Super Sized Life?

Our pastor, Bishop Michael Sloan, continuously challenges us to "Jump into the Bigness of God!"[1] What a concept; this God who is larger than the universe itself is asking us to live our lives in the same manner He lives…largely. The Bible says that He measured the earth with the span of His hand (Isaiah 40:12). Think about this, the earth reaches from God's thumb to His little finger, that's pretty big if you ask me! Another scriptural description says that the earth is the Lord's and its fullness and everything that dwells in it (Psalms 24:1). In fact, it goes on to say that God uses the earth as His footstool (Isaiah 66:1).

Living Largely

The prophet Ezekiel foretold of a time when a river would flow out of heaven into the earth, the waters would bring healing, and with that an invitation for all who desire to enter into those waters can be healed. He talks about the various levels of this river; for some it comes up to their ankles, for others to their knees; some will enter waist high waters, and then some will go into the deeper places described as waters you can swim in. Whatever level you enter, the challenge is to get into this large life with God and to keep going deeper until you have lost control and are completely saturated in the largeness of God.

Let's revisit this French fry thing. Do you have a Happy Meal mentality? As long as God forgives you, feeds you, and gives you a spiritual toy you're satisfied. Are you a Regular order of fries? You're saved, on your way to heaven, go to church and do all the religious or spiritual exercises that you're supposed to do, every once in awhile you get a little excited, but on the most part are maintaining the garden you've found yourself planted in. Or are you a Super Size fry? You have had more than an experience, you've had an encounter and are developing a relationship, not with a historical Jesus, but a right now Jesus, One who is standing at the door of your life inviting you to jump into His bigness and live largely.

Join me in the journey as we discover how to live largely!

Chapter 2

Learning to Live Largely
(Isaiah 54:1)

Have you ever wondered why movies like "Hook" or the "Chronicles of Narnia" are so popular? I love the movie "Hook", the story of Peter Pan who had grown up and forgotten how to fly; it was only when his children were carried away to Neverland by Captain Hook, that Peter discovered who he really was. My favorite part is when one of the Lost Boys grabs him by the face, looks deep into his eyes and says, "Oh, there you are Peter, it is you! Look guys, he is Peter Pan; he's just grown up and has forgotten how to fly!"

I think too many of us are much like the grown up Peter Pan; at one time we dreamed great dreams and saw great visions. There were moments in our lives when we believed for the impossible, read the Bible and believed that the same God we read about there was the God living inside of us. We believed that He could and would do anything, after all, we're His kids!

Movies like "Hook" and "Chronicles of Narnia" appeal to me because they challenge the underdog. The hero in the movies usually isn't the most popular person, in fact, most of the time they're the most normal, or the one no one would ever expect to amount to much of anything.

What makes the difference is that somewhere along the way these people discover who they really are and find a release from deep within. They allow themselves to fly and to soar, to rise above their circumstances and to live larger than life.

How do you view yourself? What do you think about your life? Is it what you want it to be? More importantly, do you really believe that you are fulfilling your God-given potential by living largely?

Some time ago I was seeking the Lord, asking for direction for the future, I heard the Holy Spirit whisper two words into my spirit: Live Largely!

I knew it was the Lord, but have to admit, was a bit intimidated to say anything about it to anyone else. Look around us, our world is in turmoil, recession has taken its toll on the economy, homes are in foreclosure, gas prices are soaring towards all time highs, people are struggling to make ends meet, and I'm going to tell them to live largely…right! As the months continued to go by, the word of the Lord within my spirit continued to grow. I heard the Lord reminding me that He is not bound; neither surprised by the conditions of our world. Nothing catches God off guard. He knows and orders our steps! The challenge of living largely isn't about going out and buying a house we can't afford and expecting God to pay for it; no, it's more about you and me allowing God to be Himself in and through us.

The thing you find in these fictional characters has also been found in multiplied thousands of believers throughout history, they are people that simply have a dream. A dream can be defined as "inner vision; the ability to see what others can't, and the willingness to go after it and make it happen." The difference between a dream and reality is YOU. Only you can take the necessary steps to obey what God is asking of you. Dreamers see what their lives could be like from the inside, their vision consumes them and propels them to reach beyond the visible into the invisible and bring the invisible into the visible. Dreamers have an ability to see what others can't, they possess an imagination that is undaunted by outside influences.

For some people that concept is quite frightening, it's not safe, and for them it's not possible because to them it's not real. Ephesians 3:20 says that God is able to do exceedingly and abundantly above that we are able to ask or think (imagine), and that it's according to the power that is working within us. God has placed the ability to dream and to think outside the box of normal within us. He is a creative God; nothing He has ever done was a duplicate. God is not a parrot that only repeats what someone else has said or done; no, God is an artist, everything He does is creative and unique, everything is an original!

How do you see your life? What are you doing to make your dream a reality? How will your life be measured? Living largely isn't about bigger things, it's about bigger people. It's about people who have discovered who they are, what God desires and is planning for their lives, and are going after it. Let there be no doubt in your mind; God has a plan for your life. He wants to reveal it to you and He wants you to see it so deeply in your spirit that your life is totally transformed (Jeremiah 29:11).

> Psalm 18:19 says, "He brought me forth into a large place: He delivered me, because He delighted in me."
>
> Psalm 31:8 states, "You have not handed me over to the enemy but have set my feet in a spacious place."

Living Largely

Outward and obvious situations do not stop dreamers. They may serve as detours and distractions, but they never stop them. I am reminded of the dreamer Joseph in the Book of Genesis. Because of his dreams his family envied him and eventually hated him. The Bible says that they sought to kill the dreamer. What they didn't realize is that you may kill the dreamer, but you'll never kill the dream of one who is living his life to the fullest. People that are living largely are people that believe that God is bigger than their stuff…and we've all got stuff.

In Isaiah 54 the children of Israel are in exile and in bondage. The prophet has been telling of the coming Messiah, he speaks of a child that will come as a sign, born of a virgin, and will embody everything they have longed for. When He arrives life is going to change forever. It sounds really good, but they're still in exile, their lives aren't exactly going as they planned. Isn't that usually where God steps in? He usually shows up right when we think He has forgotten us, and He drops His word, His plan into our spirit, and He leaves it with us to live out.

Chapter 54 is one of those places where God simply drops in and tells them that things are getting ready to change, so get ready. The chapter begins with God comparing Israel to a barren woman, one who is empty and without life. There is no seed, no life, no hope, and more than that, seemingly no future. Suddenly God comes on the scene declaring, "Sing, O barren woman, you who have not borne. For more are the children of the desolate, than of the married woman, says the Lord!"

What a word! The announcement of a new baby is life changing; it brings all sorts of emotions and contemplation, especially when you previously have been unable to conceive. The amazing thing about the Lord is that He is able to bring new life where there doesn't appear to be any life at all. The Bible describes Him as the God of all comfort and the God of hope. Jesus said that He has come to give life, and the reason He can give life is that He is life.

God wants to give you new life. There is no circumstance or situation that God cannot invade and make a deposit of life into. The creative nature of God is to come into our mess and create a miracle. In Genesis 1, the Bible says the earth was without form and was void, and darkness covered the face of the earth, and the Spirit of God moved upon the face of the waters. The Hebrew word description for the phrase, "without form and void" implies that it was a chaotic mess and then God moved and out of the mess God created order and life. He can do the same for you today.

I believe we are living in the greatest days of human history; there is a move of God in the earth, it's unlike any other move or time in our history. What God is doing today is deeper, not always as visible to the naked eye, much like when Elijah was ascending into heaven; he told Elisha that if he saw him when he went up he could have a double portion of his anointing. Elisha had to see through the stuff into the heavenly realm in order to receive what he desired. If we are to live largely we will have to be able to see past the past, live in the now, and look into the future and pull out those things God has prepared for us.

Living largely can be done by anyone, here's the key: People that live largely are people that are big on the inside! They are people that have received the word of the Lord and are allowing that word to shape their lives and to change their very existence. Let me share some simple power points as to how it works:

Living Largely

People who live largely declare their destination: This is why the prophet told Israel to Sing like a Barren Woman, it was a prophetic declaration, it was the public announcement of the word of the Lord. The scripture teaches us that we shall declare a thing and it will be established; it goes on to say that the testimony of Jesus Christ is the spirit of prophecy; and that we may all prophesy. God has, is and will speak to His children. It is a historical fact, a present truth, and a future reality, God has never stopped speaking, it's just that sometimes His kids aren't listening; we can't hear all that He has to say because of the busyness of our lives. When I speak of making prophetic declaration, I'm not suggesting that we just work something up in our minds and begin to spout off our own thoughts and personal agenda.

Prophetic speech is biblical. Isaiah said that you will hear a word from behind, saying, this is the way of the Lord, walk in it…, prophetic speech is directive, and it is God putting His desire and will into your spirit, it is growing within you until you begin to boldly declare this is what the Lord has said to me. It will change your life and the atmosphere around you! When we testify of what God has said and is doing in our lives, we are prophesying to others what He can do in their lives.

Another thing the prophet told Israel was to **Breakout in singing!** What he was telling them is come out of hiding; don't be afraid to let others know what God is doing in your life. If we are to live largely, we've got to lose our shells; those protective barriers we've allowed or those we've built ourselves to protect us from the outside. Walls don't just keep things outside; they also prevent things from getting inside.

Learning to Live Largely

I'm reminded of the story of Gideon. Israel was under a time of severe oppression, and their enemies were surrounding them and taking everything they had. The Bible says the angel of the Lord found Gideon hiding in the winepress and He called him to come out of his hiding place, the Lord had a mighty work for him. Many believers are like Gideon, hiding from their oppressors, afraid to step up and step out; worried that something will happen, fearful of failure. God wants us to break out and get free!

If you're going to live largely, you need to **Dream out Loud!** Your dream isn't meant to be hidden within you, it has to come out. Dreams cause dreamers to move, they cause them to talk, walk, and live differently. Dreams change your life and cause others to see and hear what you've got inside of you.

Proverbs 16:9: "In his heart a man plans his course, but the Lord determines his steps."

What are you dreaming about? Can you see your life differently than it is presently? Has God given you a dream? Are you telling it? Are you living it?

Dreamers and people that live largely don't wait for the perfect circumstances to arrive, rather they see every obstacle as an opportunity, and they look for potential in every situation that they face. The dream inside of them is larger than what they're facing, and the One that gave them the dream is larger than life itself. Jesus taught large living, He taught that things impossible to men were possible to God. He said that our simple seed of faith has the ability to increase when we step out and believe. Large living takes God and His Word seriously. It also requires the spirit of adventure. Remember when we were children? We dreamed of traveling to outer space, of climbing high mountains, of winning races, of driving fast cars. Perhaps it's time to dream like that again. One of my favorite "spiritual television programs" is "Star Trek." I love the introduction as the narrator talks about space being the final frontier; of how their mission is to boldly go where no man has ever gone before! I am convinced that there remains a place in God that we have yet to go. The writer of Hebrews says that we are to leave the elementary principles. In other words, we need to grow up because there are better things that accompany our salvation (Hebrews 6:1, 9). The Bible says that the eye has not seen, the ear has not heard, neither has it entered into the hearts of man the things that God has prepared for them that love Him! (1 Corinthians 2:9) In another place, it says there remains a rest for the people of God, and some must enter in! (Hebrews 4:9) Living Largely is a Choice!

As a believer I have realized that I am exactly where I want to be. As a pastor, I have come to believe that people and churches are exactly where they want to be. They may not be where they're supposed to be or where God wants them to be. They may not be fulfilling their full potential, but the choice is ours!

Those who are living largely usually don't wake up one day and find they've got the whole world in their hand. No, it starts with a word and a picture, God speaks His purpose into their hearts, they grasp it, and begin to flesh it out. Prophetic incarnation; John 1:1 says that in the beginning was the Word, and the Word was with God, and the Word was God. And the Word became flesh and dwelt among us (v. 14). The promise was given, the dream was seen, the people waited, and God came and put on a face.

Living largely means that we get the word into our spirit, we walk about it, we talk about it, we move toward it, and in time, the word spoken into our spirit becomes incarnate, it puts on a face. Churches that are exploding in growth all start out the same way, a handful of people who get a vision, dream a dream, hear a word, and they become that word.

Matthew 9, in the Message Bible, gives a perfect picture of what I'm talking about. Jesus comes into contact with blind men. Blindness is simply to be without sight; to have no vision. There are many reasons people are blind; some are born that way, some lose their sight due to accidents or physical infirmities, others lose their sight over time due to age or perhaps people and situations that obstruct their view, while others don't see simply because they choose not to. These blind men followed Jesus. They got His attention and He asked what they wanted. They responded, to receive their sight of course. "Do you believe that I can do this?" He asked. "Well of course we do!" His response amazes me, "Then become what you believe!" We will discuss this some more later.

People that live largely become what they believe!

Chapter 3

S. E. E. *(Isaiah 54:2)*

The words, "I'm Pregnant" bring about numerous emotions and responses; it goes from joy to panic all in a matter of seconds. Husbands start trying to figure what comes next while wives start planning and looking for sales on baby clothes. What follows the announcement is the most important building program in history, a baby is coming, and we've got to get the nursery ready.

The call to live largely is much like the announcement of a new baby. It is the promise of new life, the hope that things are going to change and life will never be the same again. Living largely isn't about living beyond our means; it's all about living within God's! When God gives His promise to us, we have to enlarge our hearts, to increase our boundaries and make room for what is on its way to our lives.

Jesus wants you to have an abundant life…Now!

Large living begins with a Word, a prophetic promise given to rearrange and change your very existence.

Isaiah 54:1: "Sing O barren woman!"

When God speaks a prophetic word to you, how do you respond to it? Do you take it in stride and move on doing business as usual, or do you begin to nurture and develop that word in your life? Do you prepare yourself for the maturity and manifestation of that word? Much like the announcement of the coming baby, a prophetic announcement means we allow that word to shape our very existence.

How do we respond to a Prophetic Word?

- **We recognize that it is a seed sown into our lives.**
- **We nurture and cultivate it, fertilizing it with God's Word, Good Fellowship, and Faith.**
- **We allow it to grow naturally and to be released visibly.**

I remember when we found out we were expecting our first child, we were elated! We had prayed and planned; my wife wanted to be a mother more than anything. When she discovered she was expecting it was on - life wasn't going to be the same! One day while at WalMart, I ran into a lady that had attended our church, and mentioned to her that we were expecting. She said, "Oh I know, I ran into your wife the other day and she was trying to look pregnant. She had a smock shirt on, even though there wasn't much to hide!" People that live large are people that realize that even though you may not see it immediately, the promise is within you, eventually it's going to show…so you have to get ready!

Growth is a natural thing; it's the result of relationship, of nurturing, and of intimacy. Jesus said that His Kingdom is not with observation; it's not always easy to say it's here or it's there, the Kingdom of God is within you.

S. E. E.

God has placed everything you need to become large within you; perhaps it's time to get yourself some maternity clothes and start making room for the baby!

True growth is change; true change begins on the inside. Change is a very popular topic these days; we're all talking about it, and everyone wants change in some way at some time. One of the things I find amazing is that most people want change as long as they don't actually have to change We want new life without losing the old life. If you're going to live largely you will have to change, and that change will start deep within your spirit.

Living Largely is a mindset. The Bible says, as a man thinks in his heart, so is he (Proverbs 23:7). We are what we think because what we think determines who we are and dictates what we do. Our thinking is the result of our input and surroundings, it is the creation of the environment we place ourselves in, both naturally and supernaturally. Most of us have read Galatians 6:7 that says, "Whatever a man sows that will he also reap." There's a spiritual principle here. If you don't like what you're reaping, change what you're sowing and that begins in the head and heart, as we adjust our thinking process to think more like God thinks. The Book of Philippians says we are to have the same mind as Christ, another scripture says we have the mind of Christ. Philippians 4 says that we are to think on things that are lovely and pure, things that are honest and of a good report. In today's world it's easy to dwell on the negatives, to think about all the things that could have been or that should have been, to wonder what would have been. Those who live largely think on what God says is going to be.

A changed mindset results in people who serve God and their generation by thinking on Christ, trusting Him to be who He says that He is, a big God that refuses to withhold any good thing from His children. They are people who are learning to expect Him to show up in their lives and to be Himself in us. Perhaps this is what the Bible was talking about when it says His name shall be called Emmanuel, God with us!

With the announcement of a new baby to barren Israel, God gave further instruction. He quickly moved this exiled people into a building program. You can't ask God to change your life and expect it to stay the same. You can't be pregnant and not gain weight, and you certainly can't hide it forever. When you decide to live largely you're going to have to make room for the baby!

1. Enlarge the place of your tent!

Get big on the inside! You are the tent or the tabernacle of the Holy Spirit; refuse to quash the expansion He desires to do in your life. Step up to the plate and step out by faith and allow God to enlarge your life.

Enlargement takes place when we dream big. Let me ask you a question, "What do you want to be when you grow up?" I'm afraid many people have quit dreaming, they've become old before their time, and they've simply stopped dreaming. Too many believers have accepted life as it is, status quo is a present reality, and they are no longer looking for past dreams to become the present or even the future reality.

If you're going to live largely, you're going to have to dream again, and you will need to be willing to release others to dream as well. We tell our children that they can do anything, they can be whatever they want in life…that is until they come in wanting to do something outrageous, and then we want to rein them in, redirect them, and get them to do something that is within the reach of our imagination. Perhaps we should take a page from their book and dream about things that are so huge that unless God is in it, it can't be done.

Julie and I have two daughters; both are excellent students, and both have definite ideas of who they are and what they want to be. Our oldest is attending college and will receive a business degree. In time, she may even pursue a law degree. That's quite the lofty dream. Our youngest wants to be an author. She's already collaborating with a fellow student on a book. She writes at home and draws illustrations to accompany her writing. I can't wait to see all these two girls will accomplish. Hard work combined with an internal dream will bring about the fulfillment of what is in their hearts, and you better believe that as parents we are encouraging them. We're watering the seed sown deep into the soil of their spirits.

Don't settle for less than what you know God has destined for your life. You may not get there immediately, but you will get there. In a natural pregnancy, the nine month period from conception to delivery is called "gestation." During this time the child in the womb goes through many phases and transitions until the moment of delivery arrives. Your life will take you through many places and processes before you arrive at your ultimate destination, but don't stop dreaming! Never accept a mundane life, a spirit of mediocrity, or status quo. Quit playing it so safe. Never rest at average. Don't allow fear or failure to dictate your attitude. Move beyond all of that, get up in the morning, look yourself in the face, declare that this is the day the Lord has made for you, and as you're rejoicing, start moving toward God's promise in your life...Enlarge your thinking!

Enlarging leads to stretching. Can you be enlarged? Can you be reshaped? Are you willing to expand your limitations? Stretching allows us to live extraordinary lives, large lives, lives that reach beyond our wildest imaginations.

Solomon desired to build God a house. His desire was to make God's name great, for the surrounding nations to see God's greatness, and yet, as he pursued this commendable plan, Solomon realized that no physical building would be large enough to contain this mighty God that we serve. Stretching is an exercise of our faith; it enables us to demonstrate the greatness of God in our daily walk.

> **Daniel 5:12: "This was because an extraordinary spirit, knowledge and insight, interpretation of dreams, explanation of enigmas and solving of difficult problems were found in this Daniel."**
>
> **Daniel 5:14: "Now I have heard about you that a spirit of the gods is in you, and that illumination, insight, and extraordinary wisdom have been found in you."**
>
> **Daniel 6:3-4: "Then this Daniel began distinguishing himself among the commissioners and satraps because he possessed an extraordinary spirit, and the king planned to appoint him over the entire kingdom."**

Dreamers not only see things, but dreamers make things happen...they DO things! James says that we are to not only be hearers of God's Word; we are to be doers of the

Word and Work of God. Doers create a path for others to follow; they create a life flow that affects others. If you will enlarge yourself and allow God to stretch you, God will cause you to attract favor and blessing!

> **Daniel 2:32: "But the people that do know their God shall be strong, and do exploits."**
>
> **Proverbs 3:4: "Then you will win favor and a good name in the sight of God and man."**

2. Do Not Spare

Remember a few pages back when we compared our lives to Happy Meals and Super Sized Fries? People who live largely are people who are willing to take a risk; they have a Go-for-it attitude. Being a super sized saint means living abundantly when everyone around you and everything within you says, "Play it safe." To live abundantly you have to give abundantly. This is true in every aspect of your life, whether it be in your finances, your health, your family and marriage; whatever relationships you may be involved in. What would happen if your worship became so extravagant that the fragrance of your worship filled the room and caused people all around you to be blessed? God told Israel to lengthen their cords, to remove their limits and to strengthen their stakes, to secure their place in the Kingdom and to ready themselves for the ride. After all, one can't expect to live largely without facing some huge storms, can they? Everyone won't go with you, they won't understand why you are going after God in the way that you do. They won't be able to handle the way you are stepping out and enjoying life. Your greatest opposition will come from within your circle of influence, from family and friends who like playing it safe, and from outsiders who are small minded and unwilling to stretch. Do not spare and do not be afraid, you will not be destroyed, you will grow and you will win the war!

> **Isaiah 2:2: "Now it shall come to pass in the latter days that the mountain of the Lord's house shall be established on the top of the mountains, and shall be exalted above the hills; and all nations shall flow into it."**

Chapter 4

Living Life like a Rubber Band
(Isaiah 54:2)

Life is like a rubber band. It comes in all sizes and shapes, has many uses and purposes. Rubber bands are used to hold things together, to bind things up, and they are made to stretch!

Living largely is a life that is expandable; it is a life that refuses to remain the same.

Large living like a rubber band gives you two options:

1. Leave it in its original state
2. Stretch it-move it from its present state.

One of our church members made this observation, "Faith is like a rubber band, only useful when snapped." "To live largely you have to exercise your faith or else you won't grow largely. You can't do it by yourself, it takes stepping in faith. If you stretch a little, it will only go so far, stretch a lot, it will go across the church. So the question is, "where do you want it to go?"

Stretching causes you to lose your original shape. Sometimes stretching can be a painful experience where we find ourselves pulled one way and then another. Often we see this pulling as a satanic assault, when in truth it may be the work of the Master Potter as He reshapes our lives in preparation for future expansion in life. If we fail to stretch then life remains the same; we never go anywhere, never do anything and we never grow. Jesus made a powerful observation. He said that new wine cannot be placed in old wineskins. The wineskin of that time was made of some type of animal skin. As it aged, it would become brittle and hard, unable to expand with the potent new wine being poured into it, so it would break. Is it possible that there are times when we are so fearful of breaking that we fail to allow God to make us into new wineskins? It is much easier to remain in our shape or order than it is to stretch and become a new wineskin. One of our greatest fears is that if we stretch too far we will snap.

Snapping may not be as bad as you might think, certainly snapping can have some negative aspects, and it can also prove to be beneficial. There are two aspects of snapping that we deal with:

1. It causes us to break out of our shape into a new dimension of life…God's shape for our lives.
2. We fear being broken; inside we believe our lives may be irreparable.

Many people remind me of the nursery rhyme Humpty Dumpty. Do you remember it?

> Humpty Dumpty sat on a wall; Humpty Dumpty had a great fall. All the kings' horses and all the kings' men couldn't put Humpty Dumpty back together again.

The message of the Gospel is one of reconciliation and restoration. It's about marred vessels and warped wood, people whose lives are fractured and fragmented, and it's about broken things being made whole. There are people who come into our lives that are so broken and so hurt that they believe their lives can never be repaired.

They have been stretched so far by life that they are afraid to allow God to stretch them. They question if anyone cares. They wonder what will happen if they snap and lose their shape, "Can the church put the pieces of my life back together?" By nature I am a fixer. I want people to be good and for things to go well. I struggle to make sure that lives and situations are reconciled. I want everything to work out. However, it doesn't always work out and that frustrates me. I believe that the church should be the safest place in the world, that it should be a place of peace and safety, a place of security, a place where broken things and broken people are put back together. Jesus is the Repairer of the breach. He is the One that has the ability to take lives that have stretched so far in the natural that they have snapped, and to restore them and stretch them beyond their nature until they take on His.

Let's revisit Israel for a moment. Let's take a minute to visit the exiled chosen people of God. They have been hidden within a hostile nation, God has given them a promise, and they have been challenged to enlarge and expand, to stretch and not to spare. God has compared them to a barren, rejected woman, one that is lifeless and empty. Suddenly God speaks life, change is imminent, and new life is within you! Prepare, for that change is His word. Learn to stretch, because it's going to be an incredible journey. But remember this, often before it gets better, pregnancy gets a little bit bumpy!

When a woman first discovers that she is expecting a child there is little evidence that a new life is forming within her. After awhile she may suffer some morning

Living Largely

sickness. It's the body's way of adjusting to this new life that is forming within it; this little person that requires extra nutrients and expects to find shelter there for the next nine months. Outwardly, few can see what is taking place from the outside. The stretching is gradual, begins with a little bump, and then grows a little larger, until finally some women believe they're going to give birth to a basketball. While the news of this new life is welcomed and the arrival is looked forward to, the time in between this season of stretching can be quite uncomfortable.

First of all, your shape changes, your hormones get all out of whack, your stomach may be upset, and finally, your clothes don't fit. Stretching in pregnancy is the preparation for a woman as she transitions from being a wife to a mother. Her identity is taking on another dimension, and while it promises to be rewarding, getting there has its moments.

Your stretching exercises as you pursue the large life are quite similar. They begin with a simple impartation or deposit of life. Then, your spiritual hormones get all messed up, suddenly you are moving in an entirely new direction. It can upset your spiritual stomach because your appetite will change and you will desire things now that in previous times you only desired occasionally.

The old clothes of casual, carnal Christianity will no longer fit; you're now wearing the clothing of favor and new life. What's happening is that as you stretch and grow, you are learning to wear appropriate clothing, things that allow for your expansion.

Another analogy is when you fast forward a few years. That little baby is now a little girl. One day she grows extremely quiet, you can't find her, which means she's into something. You find her in your bedroom play-

Living Life Like a Rubber Band

ing house. She's got your best high heels on, your nicest dress, your finest jewelry, and your going-out-on-the-town make up and perfume. Lipstick is smeared from one ear to the other, and when she sees you she says, "Mommy, am I pretty?" Despite the fact that she looks like Bozo the clown and that she's made a complete mess of your stuff, what's really happening is that while outwardly her body says she's a child, there's a woman inside that is growing, waiting to get out!

The same is true of us when we come to Christ; our sins are forgiven, the life and nature of God are deposited into our spirits, and we become new creations in Christ. Everything we need to become who God wants us to be is deposited inside of us. It's just waiting for us to stretch and mature so the fully developed us can come out. Living largely accentuates this. It causes us to change our focus and to live for what is most valuable, rather than things that are surface level.

Let's go back to the pregnant woman for a minute. She starts out with big news, then has some upset stomach as she transitions. From there, she begins to stretch, her skin expands until she thinks she's going to pop...but she doesn't, and neither will you. It's all a part of God's plan...you have to stretch if you're going to live largely.

Chapter 5

Change the Label
Isaiah 54:4

The Message Bible

"Don't be afraid — you're not going to be embarrassed.
Don't hold back — you're not going to come up short.
You'll forget all about the humiliations of your youth, and the indignities of being a widow will fade from memory."

Labels are important; they provide identity, information, and instruction. Without labels we can find ourselves in a world of trouble, we reach for the wrong medicine or eat the wrong food. Labels help us find the right size clothing and enable us to choose the right brand. Where would we be without labels?

Labels create illusions as well as identification. Let's say you're purchasing some clothing. You have to make a choice between two different shirts, both are similar in price, but the only difference is the label. One of the shirts is a brand name and the other is a cheaper brand. Which one are you going to buy and what is the determining factor? Is it the label? Doesn't the label insinuate something about the product that may or may not be true? For all we know both shirts were made by the same person in the same factory.

They were just offered by different companies and given labels that identify them by a brand that creates an idea of value in your mind.

As human beings we all wear labels, those things that create our identity and cause others to develop an opinion of who and what they perceive us to be. Sometimes the labels we wear are chosen for us, placed upon us in our youth, because of where we live, what type of home we live in, what we drive, the type of clothing we wear, where we work and what we do. All of these things create a persona, some of it is external and some is internal, some is social and some is religious; call it what you will, we've all got labels.

I once did an illustrated sermon on this line of thought. One Sunday morning I took a stack of identification labels and put various things on them and had them passed out. On those labels were things like depression and discouragement, addicted and angry, afraid and peaceful, frustrated and fearful, etc. I identified various emotions and expressions that people deal with every day. The people wore the labels throughout the service, shook hands and hugged necks, sang and worshiped, all the time wearing these labels so others could see them, thereby the potential to form an opinion about that person based on their label was present.

Every day we develop ideas and opinions of people based on the labels we perceive them to be wearing. They're not visible like the name tags I used, but they're there nonetheless. We perceive things about people based on our observations of them or based on our relationships with them. We decide a person is a certain way because of a conversation with them or something we hear them discussing. Some of those perceptions are correct, and some

Change the Label

aren't, but once we've labeled them, it's how we see them, right or wrong.

What about our own labels? You know, those personal items that we wear like badges and name tags, we just do it without realizing it. Our labels come from our childhood, from our relationship with our parents and siblings. They exist within our hearts and minds, affecting how we perceive ourselves and others. If a person grows up poor they may see themselves as less than those more fortunate than them, or if a person grows up in the home of an alcoholic they may believe this will be their fate as well.

Labels are either a blessing or a curse. If you wear a label that is not truly who you are, you will begin to believe that this is who you are and will begin to shape your life according to that label. If I believe that God doesn't love me like He loves another, it affects how I respond to God and that person that I perceive to be more loved. Take a person that has been abused by his father. It can be quite difficult for him to accept God as his Father because his earthly father has abused or abandoned him. This is what he expects from God and anyone He places in his life.

If you're going to live largely, you will have to allow God to help you change the labels of your life. My pastor has imparted a simple truth that is permanently embedded in my spirit, "I'm not what you call me, I'm what I answer to!"[2] This is true; we are not the sum total of where we've been or who we used to be. We are what the Word of God declares us to be. I've heard people say, "Well, I'm just a sinner saved by grace!" That's not biblical; the Bible says that if we are in Christ we are new creations (2 Corinthians 5:17). It also says that we are called to be saints (1 Corinthians 1:2). It says that we are salt and light and life. When you come to Jesus Christ, He changes your label. You are

Living Largely

no longer identified by your past life, nor your failures or your successes. You are called by His name and you are dead, and your life is hidden with Christ.

Don't allow self-imposed labels or the labels others may put upon you to identify you. Wear the label of the righteous, be who the Lord says you are.

Israel had been identified by her captivity and exile. The city of Jerusalem had lost its grandeur. It was known for what it had been, not what it was or what it was going to be. The Jewish people became identified by their captors and developed a slave mentality; forgetting who they were and what God had promised them. They bore the reproach that others placed upon them and lived beneath their means and calling, being perceived by other nations and by their captors as barren, empty, and lifeless women, incapable of creating and releasing new life.

God's promise to Israel was this, "You don't have to be afraid of anyone anymore! I am going to lift the reproach, and those that once despised you will now recognize you and respect you!" God would remove the reproach of being a barren woman and make Israel fruitful, giving her more children than those nations around her. I am reminded of God's promise to Abraham and Sarah. He said that their children would be numbered like the stars in the heavens and the sands of the seashore, and nations would be blessed because of their relationship with Abraham's family. God was simply saying, "I am going to change your label!"

I believe that God wants to change the labels of men and women who have lived beneath the weight of what others say and think about them. There are people who live in fear of the opinions of men, under the bondage of labels that have attached themselves to their minds and lives.

Christ has redeemed us from the curse of the Law. We no longer live under the fear of retribution of a powerless religious system or of the mandates of people who place unfounded expectations of us. Our lives are no longer defined by our past; we are defined and named by the Word of the Lord.

We change those labels by living largely, by allowing the Holy Spirit to impart a new heart and mind, so we see ourselves differently. When we see ourselves as God sees us, we live differently, and when we live differently others perceive us differently.

Living largely is all about experiencing inward change that results in an external expression. Everything God does in our lives begins inwardly. He may use outward circumstances to develop us but the real change always begins in our heart and mind. It works something like this: God gives us a promise; that promise grows inside of us, problems arrive to help us develop, and then the promise manifests through us and changes the atmosphere around us.

Life is filled with labels; let me ask you a question: What label identifies you?

I mentioned earlier that labels create perceptions. How we perceive a matter or how we perceive ourselves determines how we live and think.

Our perception has an effect on our attitude and actions; how we perceive ourselves dictates how we carry ourselves and how we respond to others.

Israel was perceived as a barren woman, but God's perception of Israel was quite different. He saw her as a fruitful, productive woman, one with many healthy children. God's perception of who and what you are is far greater than how others perceive you, and more importantly, how you perceive yourself.

How do we change our labels?

- Do not be afraid to change.
- Understand that change is inevitable...It will come, make it work for your favor and good.
- Remember, your identity is found in your Maker...Who's your Daddy?

Chapter 6

Got a Minute? *(Isaiah 54:6-10)*

I am an on-time person for the most part. I may be right on time; but I will be there on time. In fact, I simply despise tardiness; I think everyone should be on-time, if not early. It's just one of those idiosyncrasies that make me who I am. We all have them. The church we currently pastor begins evening services on Sunday and Wednesdays at 6:30 P.M., the Wednesday evening service is one hour. Over the past few weeks we've had some guests come in around 7:00-7:15, about the time they sit down and get settled in, I'm standing them up and sending them out...finally one week they decided to ask what time we begin.

In a perfect world people would be on time and things would move forward progressively and life would always be good. In a perfect world everyone would get along, there would always be enough money, gas prices would be cheaper, sickness would be a thing of the past, and joblessness and poverty would be history. In a perfect world all of our prayers would be immediately answered exactly like we asked, and the Lord would always move when we wanted Him to...In a perfect world.

Isaiah's world wasn't perfect and neither is ours. In fact, at the time chapter 54 was written, Israel had been in exile for around 100 years. I would imagine that during that time some people had offered up some serious prayers, perhaps some fasting took place, and some frustration had been experienced. If they were anything like people today, there were some intense conversations, maybe even some complaining, after all, these are God's chosen people, the apple of His eye, those He has promised to bless and protect; you remember God's covenant promise...I will bless those that bless you and curse those that curse you. Here, however, they are in exile, living under the domain of an oppressive enemy, and God's telling them things are going to change...yeah right!

To make matters a bit more intense, God speaks to them and reminds them that He has called them. Even though they feel forsaken and are grieving, feeling abandoned and refused, God reminds them that He knows exactly where they are and that His love and call for them has not changed.

It's that timing thing again, that frustrating attribute of God that He knows exactly where we are, what we're going through and what we really need.

To top it off, He not only knows these things, but has orchestrated every aspect of our journey with Him, allowing us to be exactly where we are, and has already developed a plan of deliverance and blessing.

To me, that's a powerful revelation, to know that God sees and speaks into the true situation, not just our imagination or perception of the matter. The facts are that sometimes life is not exactly as we see it and tell everyone it is; sometimes it's better and sometimes it's worse. Regardless of how it actually is, God is there, seeing what's taking place and seeking the opportunity to speak to us; the question is are we listening?

The amazing thing about the Lord is that He doesn't wait until life is perfect to work in our lives; He lives with us where we live and loves us, even in the storm. There's an amazing line in the book, "The Shack", the story of a man who had lost a child, was frustrated with God, disillusioned by church, and carried away to an encounter with the Lord. At one point God speaks to him and says, "The problem with people is they don't know how to live loved!"[3] I think there is great truth and revelation in that thought. How many of us are unsure of God's love for us, how often do we equate God's love and blessings with comfort and circumstantial evidence? In the Book of Job, the Bible records a conversation between God and Satan concerning Job. Satan is looking for someone to tempt, he wants to mess with his life and mind, God asks if he has considered Job. Satan's response is classic, "I would, but You've got a hedge of protection surrounding him, he won't budge!" The Lord's response is simple, "I'll take it down, just don't kill him!" Life isn't always going to be perfect. The enemy is certain to show up but God knows where you are, what's inside of you, and He won't let you face anything He knows you can't handle. I love what the Bible says about this season of temptation in Job's life, "In all of these things, Job sinned not!"

Living largely isn't a life absent of frustrations, issues, temptations and trials. In fact, when you make the decision to live largely you become a target. You become the target of people with mediocre mindsets, small minded, comfortable, in-the-box religious people, and of the devil himself. Satan doesn't mind if you remain a comfortable Christian, one that just goes to church on Sunday, complains about insignificant things, and doesn't press into the deeper life in Christ. He can use carnal believers. What threatens him are people that are willing to walk through fire and flood to get where God has destined them to go. The thing that threatens carnal, mediocre believers is on-fire Christians that are living their lives to the fullest, pressing toward the mark, and moving into new dimensions in Christ.

If you're going to live largely get ready for God to use your frailties, get ready for moments absent of the manifest presence of God...moments when it feels that all have abandoned you...even God!

Most of us have been in places where we could not feel God, when it seemed that He wasn't listening, and He certainly wasn't saying anything. To make it worse, when He does say something, it's not what we have in mind. Add to that the fact that it seems like everyone around you is being blessed, the Lord is helping them decide between Cheerio's and Corn Flakes, and you can't get a word for the most important decision in your life.

Isaiah 54:7

"For a mere moment I have forsaken you..."

Our lives are a series of seasons, periods of time constructed by God to create in us the purpose He desires to develop within us. The scripture teaches us that there is a time and a season for everything in our lives. You can't stop a season, and unless you learn the purpose of that season, you may be there awhile. Life is much like living in the Northern United States where there are four seasons:

- Winter - a season of dying, there are some things in our lives that need to die
- Spring - a season of sowing and new life
- Summer - a season of growing
- Fall - a season of reaping

Got a Minute?

In a pregnancy, there is a period of time between the announcement that a woman is pregnant and the first visible sign or proof of new life. During that time there is life and there is growth, there just isn't any visible evidence.

Our growth in Christ also requires moments of silence, seasons when God's activity isn't obvious, but He is working nonetheless.

Seasons of Forsaking
- You feel abandoned and alone
- God says, "I left you for a mere moment"
- There is an absence of the manifest presence of God
- We live by supernatural faith
- We are sustained by Who we know
- We hold onto the last word from the Lord

People who are living largely are people who are walking through the stuff, facing the storm, refusing to die, and are determined not to quit.

Deuteronomy 13:4

"It is the Lord your God you must follow, and Him you must revere, keep His commandments and obey Him; and hold fast to Him."

Jesus said that in this life we will face persecution, tribulation, and struggles. He has promised never to leave us and that He will not forsake us. So, in those moments when it appears that He is absent from our lives, when His involvement is invisible, we must continue to follow after

Living Largely

Him believing that just as quickly as our storm began it will end. God is faithful!

In 2004 I went to Kenya on a mission's trip with Bishop Mike Sloan and his family, along with Missionary Dr. John Wisner. While there we had the honor and opportunity to meet Dr. John Greene who operates an orphanage, church, and school in the city of Eldoret. This powerful man of God is one of the most humble men I've ever met. As we were talking with him Bishop Sloan asked if it would be alright if he gave him a gift. He then took off his watch and handed it to Dr. Greene.

What we didn't know was that his watch was broken and he had been asking God to supply the means for him to get another watch. God birthed something in my spirit that day, I have traveled to Kenya yearly since 2004; several times during my time there I have heard the Holy Spirit speak to my spirit to give my watch to someone, often He whispers into my ear, "Tell them I'm always right on time!"

Time is much different in our minds than it is in God's. The Bible says that with God a day is as a thousand years and a thousand years is as a day (2 Peter 3:8). This isn't to say that He measures days by years; rather it means that God is infinite. He isn't looking at His watch if we're a few minutes late, and He is never late. When we're walking through a struggle we want it to be over with now. So, can you imagine what God is saying to us when He says, "I'll be there in a minute?" What He wants to get through to us is if we can learn to appreciate the process and trust that this season has purpose. He will show up exactly when He needs to and when He arrives it will be miraculous!

Chapter 7

Winner from Within
(Isaiah 54:11-17)

By now you can tell this is one of my favorite portions of scripture and, this concept of living largely is a huge word in my spirit. I am convinced that many, if not most believers live far beneath what God desires for their lives; that the church of our times has developed a "que sera sera mentality," an attitude that says "This is the way things are, this is how it's always been, and there's nothing we can do about it."

This attitude becomes especially more prevalent as we progress from the end times to the times of the end. As we near the return of the Lord there seems to be an attitude among believers that the path has been created, that the events of this time have been set in order, and that there is nothing else for us to do but pack our bags, sit on the curb, sing "kumbaya", and wait for the Lord to return. That's not what I see when I read the New Testament! I see a church and a people who amid all the prophetic displays of natural and supernatural acts, are walking in the promise of God, living in the power of the Holy Spirit!

The Book of Joel begins with solemn warning, an enemy is coming, and he compares it to the destructive stages of crawling, eating, destroying canker worms, caterpillars and locusts. He tells the people to warn their children, the priest to sound the alarm and for the people to pray and return to the Lord. After all of this, God sends renewal and restoration. In Matthew 13, the Bible gives a parable of farmers that go to their fields only to find that someone has sown tares or weeds among their wheat, they want to remove it, but are warned not to, the reapers will take care of it at harvest time. This is the principal of duel harvest, that in the last days everything that has ever been sown will also be reaped. It is a simultaneous harvest, both good and evil seed will come to fruition and we will make a choice which harvest we participate in.

The battle we face and the wars we win all begin and end from within. What manifests on the outside is the fruit of what is taking place in the inward parts of our lives. Our enemy is an invisible enemy with external repercussions. He uses everyday events and circumstances to distract and detour us. If we win this war, we win it from within.

Chapter 54 begins with a broken, barren nation receiving a promise and a challenge from God:

- Change is coming
- Change your thinking
- Stretch

God created a picture of what His desire for Israel looked like. When He gives us a promise He creates a focal point, a word picture, a goal for us to see and pursue. This picture reshapes our mindset and changes our way of thinking. A mother or expectant mother thinks differently than a woman without a child, and so must we if we are to fulfill God's purpose for our lives.

Expectant mothers watch as their promise grows within them. They no longer think of themselves as alone, "me" becomes "we," and their life plan now includes what is to come, not just what has been.

Expectant believers are much the same. They believe that growth and release is coming, that God has something more for them, and they plan for the future. They, like expectant mothers, understand that life will be painful for awhile, but the pain will produce a new joyful life, it will be worth the struggle. In all labor the Bible says, there is profit!

Chapter 54 ends like it begins, with a promise and a challenge. It begins and ends with God seeing where they actually are, what they're facing, and how it's going to turn out.

In verse 11 He likens them to an afflicted city. One translation calls them "sad and discouraged." One of the greatest tools of the enemy is depression and discouragement, the temptation to be disillusioned, to believe that where we are is where we'll always be. To live afflicted is one thing, but to live like you're afflicted is another. There are many people that live with afflictions, but the key is that they live with them; their afflictions do not have to define them. I have a friend that was permanently injured in a car wreck; he was in his mid 30's and is now confined to a wheel chair. It would be easy for him to give up, to quit living, but he has made the choice to live life and he lives it largely. He is one of the happiest and most encouraging people I've ever met.

"Many are the afflictions of the righteous, but the Lord delivers them out of them all!" (Psalm 34:19).

God sees your stuff! He knows who you really are, where you really are, what you're facing and how it's going to work out; nothing takes God by surprise!

The purpose of affliction is development and opportunity. God uses your affliction to develop you, to recreate you and to enlarge your borders. He uses your affliction to express to others His ability to protect and provide for His children, and He uses your affliction as an opportunity to reveal Himself in power and glory.

Affliction opens the door for restoration, and restoration is the theme of the entire Bible. It's the message of God taking broken things and making them whole; God uses broken, hurting, disassembled things and makes them all new. God wants to rebuild your life with materials of excellence, with things that will outlast the stuff!

When God brings restoration into your life He is also securing your future, assuring you that what He begins He will complete. It's up to us to continue walking in the revelation of who and what He is in us. If we're going to win we also need to be teachable, able to learn from the struggle, and to allow God to be our instructor.

Many people think that because they've been around awhile and been through some stuff that they've seen it all and got it all figured out…wrong! The longer we live the more we need to learn. I've come to realize a simple truth: I need to always have a mentor and I need to always be a mentor! It's a life cycle, we should always be learning and we should always be teaching. God's promise to Israel and to us is, "I will teach your children and make them successful!"

I've heard people say in the middle of a trial, "I think God's trying to kill me!" My usual response is, "He is!" He wants the old man to die so the new creation can arise and live victoriously, but here's the present truth you need to understand: God doesn't want to destroy you, He wants to develop you. The trials He allows to enter your life are for your benefit, serving as school teachers and lessons to be learned.

One of the lessons we have to learn is how to respond to trials; do we accept what comes our way as a learning opportunity and the opportunity for God to reveal Himself in our lives, or do we blame Him for the attack? Do we accuse God of attacking us and letting Satan destroy us, or do we stand on God's promise and rejoice that God knows and loves us well enough to allow us to walk through this trial?

God's word to Israel was if anyone attacks you, I didn't send them. You have to discern the source of your struggle. Your enemy only has three tools: 1.) Accusation, 2) Deception, and 3) Temptation. He wants you to believe he is more powerful than he is, that he has the upper hand on you, and that God has sent this storm to devastate you. You need to know that no plot of the enemy will be effective.

God creates the opportunity for you to overcome right in the middle of the fire:

> **If anyone attacks you, don't for a moment suppose that I sent them. And if any should attack, nothing will come of it.**
> **I create the blacksmith...I also create the destroyer.**
> **No weapon that can hurt you has ever been forged words spoken against you won't hurt you... (Isaiah 54:15-17).**

Living Largely

The words of Job ring in my ears as I think about the way God uses affliction and struggle: "But He knows the way that I take and when He has tried me, I will come forth as gold." God knows our path; our steps are of no surprise to Him. In fact, He has ordered them and is directing them.

In January of 2010 I had a massive heart attack. Because of the severity of this affliction and the weakness of my heart I was required to return to my home for several weeks to renew my strength prior to open heart surgery in February. During the weeks prior to my surgery there were many family members and friends assuring me of their prayers and of their confidence that the Lord would be with me; it was wonderful and deeply appreciated. Every once in awhile someone would tell me that they were praying that God would completely heal me and that surgery wouldn't be necessary. I believe that God could have done that, but even though I knew He could, I also knew He wasn't going to, this was my path, it was a road I was required to travel. Sometimes our path leads beside still waters and sometimes it leads us through raging rivers. The important thing is that God knows where we're going. And when He has tried me, when He has allowed me to step into the court of affliction, the trial of our faith is what...more precious than gold? When He has tested my faith and my resolve...two things happen: (1) I shall come forth and (2) I shall come forth as gold. Are you walking through a time of testing? Is your faith being tested, or better yet, is it being proven? You can rest in the assurance that you will come through it and you will be valuable, like gold, refined and reshaped, recovered and renewed. Never underestimate the value of the season of affliction.

Chapter 8

Connect the Dots

As children most of us remember coloring books and drawing in connect-the-dots books; a blank page with numbered dots all over it. When you connected all the dots you were able to see the desired image. Life is like connecting the dots, God creates us with an image in mind; you are a complete picture in His mind. The Bible says that in the beginning God said, "Let us make man in our image and in our likeness...and let him have dominion!" (Genesis 1:26)

You were made to reflect on the earth what God has envisioned in heaven. You were made to live in dominion and to have spiritual authority in this earth. In God's mind you are a finished product; the image is set, we simply have to connect the dots!

Living a large life has to do with becoming the sons and daughters of God, of being conformed to the image of God. Outside of Christ we are marred and warped, we are earthy, but when we come to Jesus everything changes. From the inside out He transforms us to reflect the Kingdom of which we now belong.

I believe that life is supposed to be adventurous, fulfilling and fun. It should be large and filled with laughter and joy. I'm not suggesting that life doesn't have its moments, that adversity is absent from our lives. What I am suggesting is we can live above the pressure and above the fray. I am convinced that the joy of the Lord really is our strength. One of my favorite scriptures that assures us of

Living Largely

this is Hebrews 6:9 where the writer says, "I am persuaded of better things which accompany this salvation…"

There is no convincing me that believers should live their lives with their heads to the ground, bottom lips stuck out, fearful of their own shadows, afraid to enjoy living. I am convinced life should be lived largely with conviction, with a song in our hearts and a spring in our steps. The relationships we form, the jobs that we work, the places we go, should all reflect our decision to live as citizens of God's kingdom, as men and women that have defeated the devil through Jesus Christ, and are walking in the words of the Apostle John, "I would above all things that you should prosper and be in health, even as your soul prospers." Living largely is a well balanced and well lived life; it speaks of wholeness and health in every aspect of our being, emotionally, financially, physically, and most of all, spiritually. We are carriers of God's glory, the presence of God is within us, and our presence should change the atmosphere whenever we are present.

I have a philosophy about atmosphere; if I come to your house and stay a few days, your house will smell like the cologne I wear for several days after I'm gone. In my mind, if I can't smell me, neither can anyone else, so my ritual is something like this: I spray cologne all over my body, then over my face and hair; after that I spray my hands and rub it all over my face. Finally, I spray it into my hands and rub them all over. You will smell me before you see me.

There's a spiritual lesson in this; the Bible says that we are to others the savor of life or the savor of death, we smell like who and what we connect to. We can change the atmosphere wherever we go if we are willing to connect the right dots that allow us to live in a large way.

Dot #1: Connections

Connections represent people, places, and things that you enter into relationship with. Those people and things that you allow to instruct and impart into your life, who and what you allow define and shape your life.

Who do you allow to speak into your life? What are you connecting to that will create empowerment? What are you connecting to and what are those connections creating?

Connections are a powerful force in the life of a believer. It is important that we create good connections, that our first and most important connection is to God, and that we make certain to prioritize that connection. Our relationship with God is our lifeline. Jesus said, "I am the vine and you are the branches, except you abide in me, you cannot bear fruit..." What He's saying is if you don't maintain a faithful connection you won't live largely or effectively.

4 Levels of Connection

- Acquaintances-People you meet and have a limited relationship with.
- Relationships-People you are willing to pursue and invest in, develop the relationship beyond a casual acquaintance. It includes family and friends.
- Intimate-These relationships have depth and greater involvement; they are more limited in number. You cannot be intimate with everyone; it can't be open to all.
- Influence-This connection has the ability to change lives. Intimacy can create life, but influence changes life, it imparts, instructs, and inspires. Influence

speaks into others and makes a difference. When influencers speak, people listen and respond.

Each of us are connected to someone in each of these four areas in some way. There are people that we know who they are and are acquainted with. We have family and friends of whom we share a relationship with; there are intimate relationships we share with fewer people, and there are people who we influence and those who influence us.

Connections are important because they give people a sense of acceptance and belonging.

Have you ever wondered why Starbucks is such a prosperous business? Think about this, over 9 billion dollars worth of coffee is imported every year. The average American drinks 3-4 cups of coffee each day, and millions of people think nothing of paying $4.00 for a cup of coffee. Is the coffee good? Absolutely. Is it that good? Not necessarily, but it's not just about the coffee. Starbucks has created a culture for connecting. They have designed their business to make connections possible and comfortable, offering a pleasant atmosphere with comfortable seating, providing free amenities and suggesting foods that will accent their coffee choices. In doing so, they're hoping that people will come and connect, sit around and enjoy one another's company…and buy some more coffee!

Connections are important. They determine who you are. When God created man, He made him to look just like Him, but then He took it a step further when He said, "It's not good for man to be alone, let Us create for him a helpmeet" (Genesis 2:18). Jesus said that a man should leave his parents and connect with his wife and they should become one flesh.

Connect the Dots

I think it's important that we choose our friends wisely, that we teach this to our children, that we teach them to use caution and wisdom in whom they connect with and who they are intimate with. These connections create production, and we live with what we produce!

Your future is tied to your connections; those who help you connect your dots, enabling you to discover wholeness.

Good connections provide life and freedom; they enable us to accomplish our purpose and to reach our destination. Connections involve:

- Giving and receiving
- Tension and resistance

Relationships are a two-way street; they require giving and receiving on all sides. If a relationship is one-sided it isn't a true relationship, it's a business decision. In every relationship there will be tension and resistance. It's kind of like plugging something into an electrical receptacle; you want it to be in the right place and you want it to stay. You want to build relationships that last. Tension in relationships isn't harmful if it is the tension of exploration and honest searching of the hearts and motives of those we're connecting to.

A bad connection can do great damage in your life. Plug a lamp into a bad socket or use an object that has a short in it and you can burn your house down. The same is true of our connections with others. Many of us have experienced bad connections in relationships and are still bearing the scars.

> Then the man and his wife heard the sound of the LORD God as he was walking in the garden in the cool of the day, and they hid from the LORD God among the trees of the garden. But the LORD God called to the man, "Where are you?"
>
> He answered, "I heard you in the garden, and I was afraid because I was naked; so I hid." (Genesis 3:8-10 NIV)

One of our greatest fears when it comes to connecting and developing relationships is exposure. We have learned to live behind masks and walls fearing others will see us as we really are and reject us. Often this fear is based on past relationships. We hold on to the pain of bad connections.

Bad connections create a void in our lives. They so color all other relationships until we see everything and everyone through an often mistaken view. Think of some of your bad connections, things like: (a) a broken relationship with God (b) a bad connection with other people (an offense has entered into a relationship or an issue or misunderstanding) or (c) a bad connection with yourself where you've lost your identity, no longer know who you are or where you're going; your self-esteem is lost and you have lost your way.

The purpose of connections is to develop a lasting relationship that provides the opportunity for life to be shared with another. The goal is not to see how many connections you can make, but how many connections you can develop and continue in. Once we enter into good and healthy connections we are able to produce and reproduce in and through others all that God has and is producing in us. Connecting with others is about enabling others to live largely just as you have learned to live largely.

Dot # 2: Communication-Say Something

There's a great story found in I Samuel 3:1-11; the story of a little boy by the name of Samuel who has been left in the care of an older prophet by the name of Eli. This child has been entrusted by his mother to this man of God to be taught in the ways of God.

The Bible says that during this time the word of the Lord was rare, there was no widespread revelation. In other words, there was a limited amount of communication between God and man. God begins to speak to Samuel in the middle of the night, but Samuel had never heard the Lord's voice and thought it was Eli. Night after night young Samuel would go to the older man and ask him what he wanted, but Eli hadn't called him. Finally, after several nights of these encounters, Eli realized it was God trying to speak to Samuel and told him to respond the next time with these words, "Speak Lord, for your servant hears You!"

God desires to have good communication with us. He wants to speak to us in a manner that we can comprehend, and He also wants us to communicate with Him. Communication is more than words and it's more than a prayer that basically involves us talking and God listening. In our relationships with other people, be it our spouse, our children, our family and friends, co-workers, etc., communication is essential.

Communication is a form of connection; it is emotional, physical, and spiritual. Communication is:

- Interacting with others
- The transference of desire, intent, and knowledge
- Accomplished by action, attitude, and words. It is both audio and visual, what we say and do
- Involves perception
- Personal

Communication is key to effective relationships, whether they be casual or intimate, at home, church, or at work. It is important that we learn to communicate:

- Openly and honestly
- Clearly
- Continually

Perhaps the greatest roadblock to effective relationships is the inability to communicate and the belief that we are. How many times do we say one thing and mean another? Have you ever assumed that someone understood what you intended to say only to find out they didn't? Or have you ever said one thing but done another and then wondered why others couldn't relate to you?

Each of us has a personality that is unique to who and what we are, call it our emotional DNA, it's the very essence of our being. Effective living is realized when we are able to make connections by communicating who and what we are to others. Sometimes we need to ask ourselves these questions:

1. Am I communicating or am I just talking?
2. Do people hear what I'm actually saying?

3. Are my actions and attitudes louder and different than my words?

One of the greatest tools of living largely is communicating. When you discover who you are in Christ, and your life begins to reflect your belief that God created you to live largely, it becomes your opportunity and responsibility to communicate this truth with others. Communicating this isn't just telling them, "Well, you should be living like this, that's what I'm doing, look at me!"

No, it's walking it out when no one else is looking, and when they're certainly not asking. It becomes such a part of your persona that when they see you they recognize it. As you speak and live among them it is simply a part of who and what you are, the message you communicate by your lifestyle.

Matthew 13:10-23

In the parable of the Sower and the Seed, the message is never about the Seed, it's always about the Soil. God's Word is the Seed, and the Word is always good and productive. But the soil is our lives and relationships, those we make connections with. Seed must be received to prosper, so the Soil has to be receptive in order for others to receive from us. We have to create effective connections and this is done by good communication. Soil must be open to Seed. It's about the relationship between the Seed and Sower. It's a partnership. It's about the trust between the two, and trust is the result of connecting and communicating. Our words, our attitudes, our actions, our very lifestyles are all Seeds as well because we speak into the lives of those we're in relationship with everyday in many ways. What makes our communication effective is that the soil we are making deposits into is good Soil, and what makes it good Soil is that it is receptive to what we are depositing into it, and that it in turn reproduces a similar harvest.

There is no greater reward in life than to see a person that you have developed a relationship with succeed. The mission of Christ on earth was to share the message of His Father's love and to see that message lived in and communicated by those He shared with. Communication is most powerful when it is an intentional and natural action, when we live our lives intentionally, determining to express ourselves in word, action and deed, to clearly, openly, and honestly share our lives with others.

Let your life…say something!

Dot # 3 Process

I love to eat. I enjoy food and appreciate the process that makes it possible for me to do so. Now, I am a picky eater even though I eat quite the variety of food. Take me to Africa and get some chapatti (bread that would remind you of a tortilla), or let's eat chicken curry from India, or better yet, some enchiladas from Mexico. Some of my favorite food is Chinese, but there isn't anything better than some Southern cornbread dressing from my mother's house! What I appreciate about most of the foods I've just described is that none of them are fast-foods that you can get from a drive through; they all take time to create and cook, each of these foods requires a process!

Millions of dollars are spent at drive-thru windows; our hectic lives make microwaving a burrito much easier and certainly much quicker than waiting for a meal to be completed. I have to admit to you, I'm a fan of quick fixes and eating on the go, but there are some things you really don't want to microwave. If you zap a corn dog it isn't too bad, but you really don't want to microwave a pot roast or a turkey dinner. There is something about the time and process of preparing and baking a turkey dinner that makes the consumption special.

The process of art is similar. When your child does a connect-the-dots picture you are thrilled to put it on your refrigerator, but if you're paying for art you want it to be something that has gone through more than connecting dots one through twenty-five.

Process is the act of creating. It involves thought and vision, an idea and a word picture; we see it in our hearts and speak out of the depths of our hearts. It's what happens when you get a good idea and decided to act on it. Between the beginning of a project and the finished product there is that period of time called process.

In creation, God had an idea of what He wanted to accomplish; He spoke and created and then said it was good. The Apostle Paul said that God has begun a good work in our lives and will continue working on us until the work is complete (Philippians 1:6).

Connections and Communication require process; we have to initiate relationships and then learn to communicate with one another. Our life in Christ is a process; we hear of Christ, accept His offer of eternal life, and then learn to live the Christ-life. It doesn't happen overnight, and it isn't supposed to; any relationship we enter has to involve this thing called process.

One of the truths I am learning is to appreciate the process. Most of us live fast-paced lives; we start our days early in the morning and don't stop until late in the evening. In between rising and falling, our dockets are filled with experiences, from getting our children off to school, getting ourselves to work, and going from one thing to the next, to finally falling on the bed for a few hours sleep before we start the same vicious cycle all over again...process. Our daily habits define us, they shape what we call life, and they create our patterns that others recognize as our way of living.

Process is the act of getting from here to there; it's getting from "A to Z." There are 26 letters in the alphabet, most of us love "A and Z," but you have to go through "B through Y to get to Z." In our lives, living largely isn't about getting up one day and deciding, "This is it! I'm living largely from now on!" It may start there, but it doesn't end there. When you recognize that your life can be better, that you really can live largely, and that God has destined for you to do so, your process has just begun. Living largely requires an entirely new way of living and thinking. It means that we adjust the way we think, talk, and walk. We've all heard the saying, "Rome wasn't built in a day," neither do we live large lives overnight.

To live largely you have to see the vision of what your life can be like; then you have to change what you say to yourself and about yourself, and then what you say to others. Once you've started the process of changing your mind and attitude, you start changing how you actually live. You adjust things, reordering and rearranging the furniture of your life. Often it is a difficult process because you move and remove things, people and patterns that have been around a long time.

A perfect biblical example of process is found in the story of the potter and the clay in the 18th chapter of Jeremiah. The story is a word picture of how God is working in the lives of the children of Israel. In this story he describes a potter who is working on a project on his potter's wheel. As he spins the wheel, shaping and developing the work, the potter discovers a flaw, the vessel was marred, so the potter did it again, he reworked it as he saw fit. We are a work on the wheel of life, God is the potter that uses process to create and recreate us until we look exactly as He designed us to look. The work that God is doing is more than an issue of image, it's an issue of purpose, you see, our lives have a certain purpose. God will not stop working on us until we can accomplish the purpose that He has determined for our lives, so He places His promise within us, and then He places us in a certain place in time connecting us with people and things that will aid us in our journey. Throughout our lives we will find ourselves unsure of the reasoning behind the process, confused at how we can be going in the right direction with so many difficulties and struggles taking place in our lives. We wonder at the movement of people and things that enter and exit our path; we need to understand that process always deposits and distributes exactly what we need when we need it, and when it is no longer useful the Master Potter moves it out of our way.

Another aspect of process is the aspect of time. God does not view time as we do. I'm quite confident that He isn't wearing a wristwatch or checking His cell phone, God isn't carrying a day planner or an IPad around making sure everything is right on schedule. The Bible says that the steps of good men are ordered by the Lord. It also says that everything is perfect in its time. The writer of Ecclesiastes said that there is a time for everything under the sun. When God created the heavens and the earth the Bible says that each day He created something and that at the end of the day He would look at it and declare, "It is good!"

Everything in your life has purpose and that purpose also has a time. Life is all about timing. Sometimes we want to believe that we are entitled to certain things; that God and life owe us something. Here's what we really believe: we believe that we are always next in line for something great, that it's our turn for blessings and success. Process understands that it isn't about life being fair or it being your turn, it's always about it being your time. In prophetic scripture, God would issue a decree, sometimes hundreds or even thousands of years before it became a reality. This gave those who heard the prophecy the opportunity to prepare themselves for the manifestation of the promise and it also created anticipation for the future. Periods or seasons of waiting do not negate the promise; they simply enlarge our opportunity to appreciate the season called process.

Dot# 4: Journey

Life is a journey; it has a beginning and an end. Our life is the part that is walked out between the beginning and the end. When we live and where we are placed at the beginning of life may not be our choice, but how we live while we live is entirely up to us. Life is our journey!

Destiny is a word we hear about a lot these days; books have been written, sermons have been preached, and we have impressed upon our children the fact that they have a destiny. I think it's more important that we appreciate the concept of destination, the word destiny simply means fate, and it speaks of the end, of how things sum up. Destination on the other hand speaks of life and where we end up, and what we find ourselves becoming and doing. My mentor and friend, Pastor Ernest E. Brown, says it like this: **"The road of life is filled with the skeletal remains of men filled with destiny, but had no destination!"**[4] I agree; many people start out on the path but never arrive, not because there wasn't greatness or purpose within them, but because they simply didn't know where they were going, and beyond that, they never realized that they were on a journey.

I am finding that it is possible to stay on the journey not knowing exactly where I'm going or why I'm going the direction that I'm going, but understanding that my steps are ordered by the Lord. Some people have never sought God's direction, they never seek for guidance, and they just head out without any purpose. These people often find themselves sitting on the side of the road out of gas, frustrated, anxious and hungry, because they didn't have a destination.

The story of Abraham is one of my favorite examples of journey. God asked him to leave his home and family and to go to the place He was calling him to. Abraham had no clue as to where he was going or what he was going to do; all he knew was God called him. The difference between Abraham and the clueless crowd is that Abraham had a word from the Lord and he followed that word. As he walked in obedience to the Lord, the journey took him into many places, connected him with many people, taught him how to communicate, and brought him through a process until he became exactly what God had promised him.

Our journey is also about perception; do I see what is or can I see what can be? Do I always look at the outward

Living Largely

or do I see beyond the veil of outward life and possess an inward vision of a changed life?

Journey refuses to leave us where we are! Without vision and spiritual perception, we are always a step behind, never arriving, always wishing, usually complaining about what we should have done, what we could have been, where we ought to be, rather than declaring, "I am boldly going where I've never gone before!"

I am a planner; organization and structure are necessary components in my life. My desk may be a mess and it may take me a few minutes to find things if you're in a hurry, but in my mess there is organization and structure.

My family laughs at me, and if I'm real honest about it, they mock me a little because when we go on vacation I take a file folder filled with hotel reservations and confirmations. In the years before we had a GPS and smart phones, I would print out maps and directions to wherever we were going. The concept of getting in the car and driving until you're tired and then stopping and trying to find a hotel is foreign to me. I don't leave the house without a place to stay, I know where we're going, how long it's going to take, where we're going to spend the night, I've got it all under control, it's all planned out.

The good thing about this is we make good time in travel and don't have to worry about finding a place to stay. The negative thing is that it makes our time together programmed and leaves little room for enjoying the sights and discovering new places along the way. It's not that I mean to control everything and everyone; it's that I begin with the end in mind, and often, no, usually, miss the journey in the middle.

Living Largely confronts this mentality; it teaches us that we start where we are, we live life to the fullest, and when we get to the end we look back and say, "What a ride!"

Our life journey takes us places we never thought possible creating opportunities which enable us to accomplish things others have only dreamed of, and it gives us a choice...what will we do on our journey? Remember the kid in elementary school that the teacher called the day dreamer? He was the guy everyone laughed at, the teacher could never keep his attention, and we all believed would never do anything with his life. Many of those day dreamers are now the leaders in Fortune 500 companies, they are creative geniuses, simply because they allowed themselves to dream and took the journey.

We don't choose where we start or finish the journey, but we do choose how we walk it out. How? We don't choose the circumstances that come our way during the journey, but we do choose how we respond to them. Our ability to remain focused and to stay in the race is essential to winning the race; more importantly, finishing the journey. Life is filled with people that started the journey but got lost or quit along the way. Some people drop out because they grow weary, others drop out because it's too painful, while others quit because of offense and misunderstandings with others in the journey. In the book of Genesis there is a story of Joseph and his brothers where they had betrayed him many years prior and sold him into slavery and had forgotten all about him. God had raised him up to a position of prominence, second in power in the land of Egypt. During a famine his brothers come before him for provisions, unaware of who he is. God miraculously reconciles this family. Joseph loads wagons filled with food and sends his brothers back to their father with a simple word of instruction, **"Don't fall out along the way!"**

Living Largely

I think it's important that we remember that humanity is not an excuse, it's an opportunity, and it is the opportunity to live a transformed life in a hostile world. It is the opportunity for people to live large lives according to biblical principles and to respond to life differently from those who don't know Christ. People who are living largely value their relationships; they recognize that one of the easiest ways to lose their way is to allow people to hinder them. Your journey is too great. It is far more important than the distractions that come when you allow people to detour you.

There will always be misunderstandings and offenses; they come with relationships, but people that are living the large life are bigger than their distractions. Let me help you with something; people are important, Jesus loves people, even those that get on His last nerve, even those that put Him to death. The frustrating truth is, many of those people that we struggle the most with are the very people God has into our lives for two reasons: (1) for them to stretch us; and (2) for us to love them. Many years ago I was a counselor at a Junior Youth Camp in the Chicago area. One of the little boys in my cabin was from the inner city and he was tough and challenging. This child got on my last nerves, he poked people with forks, he rebelled and got me all worked up. I remember one night he was in trouble and we were headed back to the cabin. I had taken all I was going to take. He told me he wanted to go home and I told him I wanted him to go home. By the end of the week I think we were both glad it was over, but a few weeks following camp I received a letter from this little boy. He wrote to thank me for making his week fun and for showing him love. He said that at first he wanted to leave but was glad he had stayed; he had asked the Lord to come into his life and couldn't wait to return to camp the next year. Along the way we will meet frustrating people and we will be frustrating people to others; we just cannot afford to fall out along the way. When believers fail to forgive others, when we fail to live peaceably with one another, we say to an unbelieving world that there is something God cannot do…He can't control His kids! God uses our journey to reveal His grace to an unbelieving world. He uses our actions and attitudes to enable people to relate to Him. He wants them to know that even though the journey isn't always easy it is worth it and it is possible to live an abundant life…even in difficult days.

There's a sign in the elevator at the Provena Hospital in Urbana, IL that says: "In the case of an emergency, you may be asked to evacuate the elevator to make room for a patient. Please be understanding, people are our business." People are God's business and they are our business too! Our journey cannot be completed without involvement with others; it's the incredible power of partnership, and the power of assembly and agreement. Jesus said that where two or three assemble together in His name or authority that His presence is there, and went on to say that when two or three agree as touching one thing it will be accomplished. It's important that we develop relationships with others on the journey that enables us to encourage others, to build one another up and to speak life into one another. The journey is much easier when we don't try to take it alone.

I have an incredible desire to live; if it's up to me I'll live to be 103 and my wife will live longer than me. We will enjoy our golden years together, living largely, rejoicing in all of God's provision for our lives. We don't want to be a burden for our children or by then, grand and great grand-

Living Largely

children, but when our time to leave this world arrives I want people to say of us that we went out living largely! You can't leave large if you don't live large. Your time for large living is now…right now! The journey you have been placed on is an incredible journey; it will be what you make it, you decide how you face opposition, how you respond to God's call and what you do with what comes your way. I want to live victoriously…today!

Chapter 9

Living Now in the Now

When I was a little boy I wanted to be like my Dad who was a tree surgeon. My Dad knew the names of most every tree we ever saw, and if he didn't, he made something up that was believable to me. My Dad could drop a tree between a house and a garage and never scratch either one of them; it was incredible. I remember watching him climb the trees he was going to prune; he called it "topping them." He would strap these spike things on his legs and go up the tree, and he never seemed to be afraid. As a little boy he took me with him, even when I was a few months old. I grew up cutting trees, dragging brush, hauling logs. I thought that's what you did on weekends and in the summer. My mother says when I was small she would hear things falling in the kitchen, only to come in and find the kitchen chairs "cut down," and me wearing my Dad's boots as I was cutting the kitchen down. I remember wishing that I could climb those trees and use the chain saw; it seemed like that day would never come, and when it did, I was one happy man.

When I read the Bible, I feel the same way as I did when I watched my Dad. I want to walk with Abraham and try to count the stars. I want to hang with Moses and watch the waters part. I really want to be with Joshua; he's my favorite Old Testament figure. He was a man of conquest and faith. Joshua, in my opinion, was the ultimate in large living. Once, he and a friend were asked to accompany ten other friends to spy out some land that God had promised them. It was supposed to be a great place flowing with milk and honey; a large and prosperous place. These ten men went into the land and it was indeed everything that God had said it would be and more. They saw people carrying grapes that were so large that it took two men to carry them but there was some opposition there. They saw some huge people (giants in the land), and the Bible says it caused the hearts of the men to sink. They came back saying, "It's everything God promised, but we better not enter the area, there are giants there!" Ten of the twelve men agreed it looked good but the giants were bigger than their faith. Suddenly these people that had spent forty years in the wilderness with God's supernatural provision were afraid to possess what God had promised them. All of these men, with the exception of Joshua and Caleb, had a negative report; the giants became bigger than their God. Joshua and Caleb said, "It is a great place and there are some issues. You guys are right, there are some giants in the land and we are well able to possess the land. We need to go in at once and take what God has promised us!"

    I love what Mark Batterson says about the Bible. He says, "It's not a history book, it's his-story; it's the story of God, the revelation of Jesus Christ to humanity. The Bible isn't an encyclopedia of what God did; it's a living book that reveals what God does."[5] How I long to live as these men and women did in the scriptures and we can! The giants of the faith we read about weren't super-duper, willy-whopper saints, but ordinary people with everyday struggles just like any of us. They were people that had issues and yet they possessed lands, took over cities, and obtained the promises God gave them. So what about us?

Living Now in the Now

One day as I was praying I heard the Holy Spirit whisper a word into my spirit. He said, "People are great about possessing My promises; they're just not good at possessing the land!" We love to read the Word, go to church and hear all that God promises us. We sing about it and talk about it. We're waiting on God's promises to manifest in our lives. We're looking for the Lord to come, either into our situation or to take us out of the world; to deliver us from our struggle. God never intended for us to develop an escapist mentality, neither did He intend for us to spend a lifetime writing all of His promises in a book and to become promise collectors. He gives us promises in order for us to possess them. He wants you to possess your promised land!

In the New Testament, Jesus introduced the concept of the Kingdom; a literal Kingdom, a Future Kingdom, and a spiritual Kingdom. He taught that you don't have to look for the Kingdom, it is already here; in fact, He said it's inside of us. The Kingdom is the authority or dominion of God lived out in the everyday lives of men. It is born-again believers possessing all that God has promised, living in this earth according to Kingdom principles as outlined in the scriptures. It's everyday people that possess the promise, the power, and the purpose of God in their lives. It's people that make this their life prayer: "Let Your Kingdom come and Your will be done in earth as it is in heaven!" This prayer is you and me asking God to let life be in this earth as it is where He is, bringing heaven into the earth. It is the fulfillment of Romans 8:19, where it says that the earth is waiting for the manifestation of the sons of God to appear. People are looking for spiritual reality, not just lite living in the name of the Lord.

Living Largely

Spiritual living, Kingdom living, Large living is about normal people living in a normal world serving a supernatural God and living naturally a supernatural life. God is not a magician that pulls spiritual rabbits out of a hat. He isn't a Sears catalog where we look through the book bending the pages that show what we want. He is sovereign and supernatural. He is beyond the limits of nature and human nature. He is able to accomplish more with one word than we can accomplish in a lifetime. What God has promised is that we as believers can do and accomplish the very same things Jesus did while on earth and more: this isn't mystical or spooky; it's the natural result of living in relationship with Christ.

I think many believers have lived their lives at two extremes; they are either so conservative and traditional that they live in the safety zone, or they live so extremely that people think they're flakes because they themselves cannot live up to their own reality. I'm convinced that it is possible to live in the presence of God and to walk in the Kingdom...now! You can overcome the obstacles of this life. You can be blessed and overcome the spirit of poverty in your life. You can operate naturally in supernatural power. It's already inside of you, just let it out!

What Jesus came to do in the life of people was not to create a super human. It wasn't His intention for believers to be robots or some type of super hero. Look at some of the people God has chosen to use throughout history: Abram was a great man of faith, but he would lie in a heartbeat to save his own skin. Elijah dealt with depression. Peter struggled with anger issues, liked to fight, and sometimes used some quite colorful language. The Apostle Paul had a thorn in his flesh, an issue he couldn't resolve, and yet, he wrote two-thirds of the New Testament. God uses ordinary people that understand that He loves us, even with our frailties. In fact, it's our frailties that make most useable because like Jesus we are able to relate to the people around us.

> **Now that we know what we have—Jesus, this great High Priest with ready access to God—let's not let it slip through our fingers. We don't have a priest who is out of touch with our reality. He's been through weakness and testing, experienced it all—all but the sin. So let's walk right up to him and get what he is so ready to give. Take the mercy, accept the help. (Hebrews 4:14-16 The Message)**

As a new follower of Christ I remember watching people that had served the Lord for years. They were mature and seemed to easily overcome issues. It appeared that they had few if any struggles and I so wanted to be like them. I had struggles; some of the sins of my past still intruded into my present, the enemy of my soul invaded my life and thoughts quite often, and I thought there was something wrong with me. What a relief it was when I found out that those mature believers that I was observing still had issues. They had simply learned to keep walking and were not allowing their issues to have them. When I read the Bible, I read of the great feats of men and women that had faced severe trials and had overcome. Women like Rizpah, whose sons had been hung and she placed a blanket on a rock refusing to leave the site until they received a proper burial. Men like Moses, who would rather see the invisible and face the impossible than to be named the son of the Pharaoh. As I

Living Largely

read the New Testament, I saw the incredible faith of men like Simeon that heard that the Messiah was coming and refused to die until He did. I wanted to experience the power of God as they did. Living in the Kingdom is living in the domain of God. When we live in God's arena, following after Him, obeying His Word and seeking to be like Him, we can and will experience the presence and power of God in our lives. It's His promise!

Are you ready for the key? Quit living as one that cannot hold his head up for fear of sinning and lift your eyes to the Lord and remember that you belong to Him! Living largely isn't a lack of humility, neither an absence of struggle, nor a guarantee of untold riches on earth. What it does promise is abundant life here and now. It does promise the supply of all your need. It does promise that any weapon your enemy creates to destroy you with will fail. It does process your access into God's presence, and that presence promises your joy will be full, which means that you can live a successful life on this earth...now!

I think we forget that God has reconciled us to Himself, and with that reconciliation we have been given Kingdom access to things that others cannot fathom. This ministry of reconciliation also gives us the position of an ambassador, one who represents another. Not only do we represent Him, we are given the authority of His name and the enablement of His power; we have been given the keys of the Kingdom! What is it that keys do? They unlock doors and open gates, and give us access to things hidden from others; we are ambassadors of the Kingdom!

Living in the Now causes us to realize where we are in human history. We live in between where we were and where we're going; it's the place between the past and the future. In this present world we live as pilgrims, pioneers, and strangers. We are discovering new places, seeking new opportunities, and leading others to the Kingdom. We are creating new paths for others to follow and modeling the life of a King's kid. Our future is both certain and uncertain; we know where we're going but are unsure of all the future holds. We have been given a glimpse of what is ahead, but are reminded that we see through a glass darkly, that we speak and prophesy in part, waiting for God to bring us into a place of perfection.

If we live in the past we miss the opportunity for a personal relationship, for our own new experiences, and if we fear the future and refuse to go there, we then chose to allow our present to be much like our past, lifeless and behind us. God wants us to life now, to believe today, to walk in present truth, to hear His voice for ourselves, and to prepare for a wonderful and outstanding future.

So how do we live in the Now? How do we enjoy all that God has destined for our lives? Is it possible to live largely in a failing economy, a war torn world, and a postmodern society where everything is questioned and nothing seems to be absolute? I believe it is. In fact, I am convinced that while we watch the dollar falling, hear the rumors of war and feel the hopelessness of people all around us that we can live victoriously, right here, right now…today!

Take a quick trip with me through I Peter 5:7-9 where Peter is addressing some church members that have been going through some stuff. They feel abandoned and wonder if God knows where they are. They've been persecuted for their choice to follow Christ. The opposition is from the world around them, both inside and out. Persecuted by unbelievers and pressured by the religious world, these Christians must have been saying, "This isn't what I

Living Largely

signed up for!" The Apostle Peter steps up to the plate. You remember Peter, the cussing, angry disciple who cut off a guy's ear? Peter writes three powerful truths to these people that give us incredible insight today:

- **Don't carry it, cast it on Him**
- **You do have an enemy after you, don't live unaware, act like you know what you're doing**
- **You're not the only one struggling, there are others, so resist the urge to quit and the enemy**

Years ago I met a retired pastor named John Daffe, a powerful man of God, who pioneered churches in the Dakota's and was well respected by those that knew him. I met him at a ministers meeting in South Dakota, while he rode with my friends and I back to North Dakota in a Volkswagen Bug. Pastor Daffe had suffered a stroke and was partially paralyzed on one side, causing him to move a bit slower physically, but it didn't detour him one bit spiritually; he was a giant. I remember we got into the car and he said we needed to pray before we left. I thought we would ask God to bless our travels. Not Pastor Daffe; I thought a revival was going to break loose. We went to Mt. Rushmore. He couldn't go up the incline so he opted to remain on a bench at the bottom of the hill. When we came back he wasn't where we left him. He was walking around praying and talking to God out loud in the national park. He was living largely in the Now!

The Bible says that God is present with us now and that He is a present help in the time of trouble. It's not a matter that He will come; He has come, is right here, right now, and He will come in the future. God is not distant, nor is He ignorant of our lives. God has already gone before us preparing the way and is now walking with us, leading us into new dimensions in Christ.

We make the choice as to how we will live. Will we make each day His day or will we live in the past wishing for a better future? How can we enjoy the future if we can't leave the past long enough to live in and enjoy the present?

Some time ago I read a powerful book called, "The Present,"[6] which was a story about a young man who learns the value of living in the now. This young man is taught about the present by an older gentleman who helps him to understand that we should appreciate the past, prepare for the future, but live in the present. How often our conversations lean backwards. We spend great amounts of time discussing the past and thinking that life would be better if we could get back to that place in time. Take a quick trip through the scripture and you will quickly find that everything in both the Old and New Testaments are about progressing, about moving forward, and about pressing toward the mark. Today is the day of salvation and now is the accepted time. God has placed us in this particular time in history; it is a "Set Time" for each of us to serve Him and to fulfill His purpose for our lives.

Set times are like appointments in a day planner; they have specific elements and purposes, and are established for us to meet with God and to represent Him to others. It's like going to the doctor or to meet someone for an important business matter; the timing is important. Set times not only affect our lives but they also affect the lives of others. Galatians 4:4 says that when the fullness of time was come, God sent His Son! There was a set time in history for Jesus to come. He was not early, nor was He late; He came at the exact moment in history set for Him before the foundations of the world. Have you ever heard the phrase,

Living Largely

"Timing is Everything?" You and I live now, today, at this present moment. It is important that we learn to enjoy the now; to live every moment that we have in full confidence that God has placed us here and that no one else can take our place.

When I was younger I loved to sleep in. I remember the seven years I served as a traveling evangelist. We would often stay up late with the pastors and then sleep until ten or eleven o'clock in the morning. As I've aged and added children to my responsibilities I have become a morning person. My father used to say that if you were in bed at 9:00 A.M., half of your day is wasted. I always laughed and told him that 12:00 P.M. was the half-way point, but now I kind of agree. It's important that we don't sleep in on life; that we listen to the words of Paul and "awake out of sleep!" Today we have two decisions to make: 1) Are we going to live in the present? 2) Are we going to live largely?

I wonder what would happen if our lives were not so deeply affected by circumstances and emotional issues? How much better would your life be if you lived with your eyes wide open and were determined to walk larger than life? Don't be satisfied to just get by or to settle!

When Abram was 100 years old and his wife Sarai was 90, God told them they were going to have a baby. After they got over the shock they quickly found out that God's timing and our timing are quite different. There was 25 years between the time God gave the promise and the birth of Isaac; what happened in between that 25 year period is rather interesting. Here they are carrying this promise around inside of them, things don't happen quickly enough, so Sarai decides that rather than waiting she will give Abram her handmaiden Hagar. Well, Hagar conceives and gives Abram a son named Ishmael but Ishmael isn't the son God promised, and in time Sarai has Isaac. After some time there is conflict between Isaac and Ishmael and between Hagar and Sarai. Sarai tells Abram, "Get rid of her and your son!" The problem with impatience is that we have to live with whatever we produce. It wasn't that Ishmael was a bad person; he just wasn't the one God had promised.

Sometimes we get ahead of God, try to help Him out, and the result is that we produce things in our flesh that follows us the rest of our lives; what is supposed to be a blessing becomes a painful reminder of our impatience and a bitter symbol of settling for less than what God intended.

Your now moment is an awareness that you are exactly where you're supposed to be, doing exactly what God intended, and that you will reap the blessings of your faithfulness. What I've found out about now moments is that usually they don't announce themselves, they just happen. One of the things that we often look for is a dramatic moment announcing the arrival of God's promise, but the truth is that usually it's while we are simply living life that we discover we're right in the middle of it. There's a story of ten lepers that came to Jesus asking to be healed. He tells them to go show themselves to the priest and as they were on their way they discovered they were healed. I think it's quite possible that while we are simply doing what we know to do, while we're living in the now, that God will release His promises into our lives.

The thought that we can live in God's presence and power now shouldn't be foreign to us. God is omnipresent, He is always here and always there, God is everywhere all the time…even now! If God is here now, then His presence and power are available to us and able to release His promises into our lives. Is it possible that we don't always recognize His nearness, that we await some magical moment or magnificent moment when in truth He is within us, waiting for us to allow Him to work in and through our lives?

You see this attitude in church often, when the service is operating in a certain manner, when our criteria for a good service is fulfilled, we say, "the Lord is here, He's moving right now!" What we really need to say is, "The Lord is present and we are aware of His presence right now!" God is always in us and with us, and we need to learn how to recognize Him and practice His presence in our daily lives. There are times when God's presence is overwhelming, we can't stand, or we rejoice or weep; while at other times there is no feeling, you just know that God is with you and you live in that love and presence and your walk of faith releases you to live out God's word…now!

Consider the words of Paul to the Philippian church, "Celebrate God all day, every day. I mean, revel in him! Make it as clear as you can to all you meet that you're on their side, working with them and not against them. Help them see that the Master is about to arrive. He could show up any minute! (4:5 The Message). The prophetic truth here is that God is present and God is coming, He is always with us so we are to live our lives celebrating God's goodness, telling others what He is doing in our lives, prophesying of what He can do in theirs and never forgetting that He may show up in person at any moment!

People that have faced near death experiences often return with a zest and zeal for life that is unlike their prior life. As believers we have been raised from the dead and have been changed by the life of Christ and are living forward looking toward the future. Our future is secure, our hope is in Christ, our foundation is His Word, and our lives are right here and right now!

Chapter 10

Living Larger than Ourselves
(Isaiah 60:1-2)

The future awaits us—God has promised a glorious end and a fantastic new life. As we await the return of the Lord Jesus Christ we are faced with both an opportunity and a choice. Either we can possess the land that God has promised us, living largely and boldly going where we've never gone before or we can sit back and wait for the Lord to come, hoping to escape the tribulations facing our world. The choice is ours!

I choose to accept the invitation to live largely and to take advantage of the opportunities before me. There is an awaiting generation that is dependent upon my present obedience, a generation that has yet to witness and experience the glory of the Lord for themselves. Our children, like many children before them in previous generations, live in a difficult time. Many have declared this a hopeless and terminal generation, one that is in danger of losing truth and biblical values.

This is also a generation that can change the world. All they're asking for is:

Authenticity-They are looking for us to be real.

Authority-They are in desperate need for leaders and mentors

Living Largely

Audacity-They want someone to challenge them wildly, to do something greater than themselves. They want to stretch human limitations and experience new horizons in Christ.

God has divinely set us up to live in this specific time and place in history. In doing so, He has given us the opportunity to share the life and divine nature of Christ with others. Scripture describes the life of a believer as light and salt. We are also described as living epistles, known and read of all men. In essence, we are conveyors and demonstrators of the life and love of God; we are living Bibles. So let me ask you a question, "What are they reading when they read our lives? Do they see people so totally in love with God, so completely consumed by His life in them or do they see people just eking by, not much different than before their conversion? I am convinced that we are supposed to be so totally different that people who have known us for years barely recognize us!

If we as believers and followers of Jesus, people infused with the presence and power of the Holy Spirit, do not demonstrate the life God's Word describes, then those around will look for the genuine and potentially fall for the counterfeit. When deprived of the genuine you become vulnerable to the deception of a watered down, anemic counterfeit. When people fail to experience the authentic, they will call anything divine!

Scripture teaches that Satan, the enemy of our souls, often transforms himself into an angel of light. What this means is that he comes looking like the real thing, making the promises that we want to hear, creating a false hope, and promising something he can't deliver. The problem is that if we haven't experienced the real, we'll fall for the imposter. A friend of mine once told of how that he dated a young lady that had a twin sister. One night the sisters decided they would see if he could tell the difference between them, and it almost worked. At some point in the date, the "other sister" messed up, and my friend recognized the imposter. God wants us to know and love Him, to be aware of Who and What He really is. He desires to protect us from deception, and we must protect a lost people from the deceiving devises of the enemy.

    Satan has taken advantage of the technology and advancement of our time by causing us to believe that intellectualism and technology (all the bells and whistles we enjoy in our time) are equal to the power of the Holy Spirit. He wants us to believe that these things in and of themselves will cause people to come to Christ. I believe these things have their place in our ministries and that they can help enhance our worship experience. I believe the church is to be modern in its approach, but these things in themselves will never replace the presence of God in our lives. Our enemy would love for us to reduce the supernatural power of the Holy Spirit to a story told of what God did in days gone by or to believe that God no longer works in this manner today. He wants to push the Holy Spirit to the fringes and to cause us to depend upon human ability and man-made strategies to advance the Kingdom of God.

    I am convinced that there will be a remnant generation that will pursue an authentic supernatural relationship with God. They will live and walk in the power of the Holy Spirit, with the belief that we cannot live by power or might, nor by intellect or human intuition, but by the Spirit of God. This must be a core value of the end-time church.

    The prophet Isaiah prophesied that Zion could not shine with her own light, but she was to reflect the glory of

Living Largely

God, a transcendent radiance, a light that reaches beyond the darkness of the times.

Darkness is all around us; it prefers deflection rather than reflection. It causes things to be covered and concealed rather than reflecting and revealed. The darkness hides the truth, burying it in the past, covering it with issues, and causing men to lose their way. Our world is dark. We live in some of the most difficult times known to mankind, where people are confused and struggling, and frantically searching for someone to help them find a way of escape. Many years ago I dreamed that I was in a dark maze in the basement of our church. I was angry and frustrated, because I kept bumping into the walls. Finally I asked the Lord why this was happening. His response was simple, "I'm sending others to you that have experienced the same thing and now you will be able to help them!" At that point in my dream I found a stairway and went up and found myself in the balcony of the church. As I was calming down someone came to me and declared the Lord had sent them, that He had told them I would know where they were and what they were going through. The darkness is all around; we must reflect the light of God's life lest others be swallowed by the darkness.

Isaiah's prophecy declares that a deep darkness will cover the earth. It will be a unique darkness; one that pelts down on the people. This darkness will attach itself like a damp blanket, depressing and oppressing the people, causing them to lose sight of the reality of God's love.

What is our response you may ask? What can we as believers do in the face of these difficult days? How do we defend ourselves and protect our world? How can we bring deliverance from this evil crisis of evil?

> "Arise, shine; For your light has come! And the glory of the Lord is risen upon you. For behold, the darkness shall cover the earth, And deep darkness the people; But the Lord will arise over you, And His glory will be seen upon you. The Gentiles shall come to your light, And kings to the brightness of your rising" (Isaiah 60:1-2).

This light is the promise of the glory of the Lord manifested and released in the lives of God's people. It is the divine nature and awesome presence of God that is revealed through us. This light that is promised comes to us, not from us; it's not ours, but His. God's presence in and through our lives is the result of an intimate relationship; the hunger of people consumed with loving Jesus. As we draw near to Jesus, His light shines through our lives and brightens the darkness, creating a path for others to follow.

This is the path of the supernatural power of God!

How do we live supernatural lives naturally in this world?

- **Understand it is the technology of the future**
- **By manifesting the authentic power of the Holy Spirit**
- **By facing the darkness...not fearing or fleeing from it**
- **By telling the Good News that Jesus is the Light of the world**

Living Largely

The good news is that God is still working in the lives of men and that there is nothing too hard for the Lord to do. In fact, as you read the scriptures you will find that some of God's greatest miracles are birthed out of crisis; they come when it looks like it's all over. The word "crisis" means "a time of threat or extreme danger." It is a turning point in the course of something; a moment of decision when a choice is made. Crisis is a life or death moment; something is going to progress or end. I've learned that it is the moment of crisis that determines what type of miracle that we need. Sometimes we don't know what to do or how to pray. We know that we need something, but aren't able to explain what it is exactly. In these times of crisis God enters the picture and works the exact kind of miracle that we need.

Modern darkness is on a roll. It senses that the normal church, the casual believer, is in retreat mode. Darkness thrives when believers retreat. It grows as we become accepting and excusing of it. So what can we do in this present darkness?

New beliefs must replace those that have diminished the reality of the Holy Spirit. Our beliefs have consequences; what we believe determines what we do and who we are. I'm not suggesting the abandonment of the absolutes or that we forsake foundational truths. I am suggesting that our beliefs must be fresh and biblical and open to doing old things in new ways. We've all heard this saying, "The message never changes but the methods for conveying it do!" God is creative in nature. His word to us is this: **"Do not remember the former things, nor consider the things of old. Behold, I will do a new thing..." (Isaiah 43:18, 19).**

Living Larger than Ourselves

Our response to the darkness of this world is an invasion of light! Jesus said that we are the light of the world, cities sitting on the top of hills that illuminate the darkness (Matthews 5:14). My family and I went to the theatre to enjoy some family time together. The room was pitched black. We were looking around trying to find a seat but couldn't see where the seats were. I took out my cell phone and the light from my phone illuminated the area enough for us to find a place to sit. Can you imagine what would happen if Christians around the world would allow the light from within them to come out?

When we allow our lights to shine we are cooperating with the Holy Spirit in accomplishing the call of Christ. Living largely isn't just about you! It's about being transformed personally and sharing what God has done in your life with others. Without light the world relapses further into darkness.

The gospel is about introducing a dark world to a new reality, about invading darkness and inviting people to enter another realm of life. Are you willing to challenge the darkness? Unless we challenge the darkness people in captivity will never be unchained. Unless we let the light of God's glory be seen through us, people in bondage remain slaves to their sin and their situations. We have seen the Light and now that light resides within us and the responsibility to shine that light is ours.

People that live largely are members of an army; a collective unity of light bearers that intentionally penetrate the darkness, searching the crevices of their world and seeking to illuminate the lives of hurting people. How many people do each of us know that are struggling? Do you have a family member or friend that needs a miracle?

Living Largely

One of the reasons many do not believe in miracles is that they have never seen one. When you read the scriptures, one of the ways that Jesus often entered the lives of people was by doing miracles. That same power resides within us, not to draw attention to ourselves or to receive glory for what we've done, but to cause others to see Christ for themselves. The miraculous is still available today. God still does seemingly impossible things. He still empowers believers to accomplish incredible feats in His name!

"Declare His glory among the nations, His wonders among all peoples" (Psalm 96:3).

We serve a God that is greater than anyone or anything. This humongous God is greater than the darkness, greater than our enemies, greater than demonic powers, greater than our sickness and disease. God is not only great, but He is also able to do exceedingly and abundantly above all that can ask or think (Ephesians 3:20). So why should the church operate in less power than the one we represent? I believe that Jesus is coming back for a powerful church, not one weakened by the darkness, one whose power is waning because of fear of present day events. We have to live larger than ourselves!

Chapter 11

Going to the Next Level
(1 Kings 19:19-21)

There's a lot of talk these days about going to the next level. I have several books and some sermon series on the subject. I admit that these things have influenced my writing of this chapter. With that said, the concept of going to new levels also connects with living largely. It is impossible to live largely and remain at the same place in life that you have always been.

When you talk about living largely you are accepting God's challenge and making a choice to live your life as God intended. It's about life change, moving from where you are to where you're supposed to be. Living largely involves connecting various important dots, understanding who we are in Christ, and doing our best to become what God says we can be.

Life is transitional; it's always moving and shifting. The very nature of God Himself is progressive, even though He doesn't change in personality or definition. God is constantly challenging us to move forward and upward. He creates the opportunity for us to progress and grow.

Next level living isn't just about experiences or encounters, but it's also about life change and maturity. Many people never realize what God has destined for their lives because it is easier to remain where they are than to climb the hill! I like what John Maxwell said about going to the next level: "The road to the next level is always uphill!"[7] It is this uphill life that leads us to new levels and higher dimensions in our walk with Christ.

Rich Rogers in his book entitled, "Next Level Living," said that the next level is when you are at your best![8]

Why would anyone want to accept mediocrity when they can have excellence?

Next level living requires effort; it understands that it is a life to be pursued. The next level for your life doesn't try to elude you, it's available to you and there for you. Sometimes we live as if this type of life is beyond our reach, as if God is just teasing or taunting us. Nothing could be further from the truth. This is the life Jesus died for, a life beyond your current level. The question is, "Are you willing to go there?

You could compare next level living to window shopping; you walk past what someone else has or is doing and wish you could do the same. We watch others worship, and see others prospering and wonder "Why not us?" God, on the other hand, looks at us and says, "Yeah, why not you?"

Take a trip through the scripture and you will find men and women that experienced next level living. You will find people that experience outlandish miracles and life changes. Whenever they met Jesus they were faced with a decision; do I want to stay where I am or do I want to be changed? In every instance that they accepted a life change, they also experienced a new level of living. They went from sinner to saint, from broken to whole, from death to life, God refuses to leave us where He finds us, He wants to take us to new levels.

Let me ask you a question: If your life was a ladder, what kind of ladder would it be?

Going to the Next Level

Would you be a step ladder? This is the type of ladder that gets you within your reach where you don't have to stretch much, just a little, it's pretty safe. Would you be a bridge ladder? A bridge ladder may give you some height, but it also keeps you leveled, on an even keel. Bridge ladders are necessary, sometimes we need to level out things that are out of balance, but this isn't the place you want to stay. Would you be an extension ladder? Extension ladders enable you to increase your ability to ascend to higher planes, allowing you to go beyond the limits, and to extend beyond your normal.

Elijah learned about next level living by experiencing a victory and a mental defeat. One day he calls fire down from heaven to consume a water soaked sacrifice. The next day he is running for his life from Queen Jezebel. He finds himself alone, asleep on a rock, and depressed.

Some of our greatest victories lead us into our greatest struggles. It's the success syndrome - what builds us up also brings us down. What has to happen is that we learn that it is essential to our well being to experience highs as well as lows. The reason I believe this to be true is that each level of our lives has a purpose. When that purpose is complete there is a lesson to be learned and then a next step to take. If there is no struggle, we become willing to remain where we are. It is easy to believe we've got this figured out and we reduced our dependence on God. So we walk in the miraculous and then experience a valley. What we need to remember is that while the mountain is miraculous, the most plush and fertile soil is in between the mountains…in the valley. The valley is a place of preparation for the next level. Never fear the valley!

While in this slump, Elijah encounters God in a huge way. First, the angel of the Lord appears to him and brings him food. God's provision for our lives never ends. He always knows exactly where we are, what we need, and how to get it to us. Then Elijah hears the voice of the Lord. What is amazing about this story is that he finds God in places he would have never looked. Elijah looked for God in the places that he had always found him, in the familiar place, but God wasn't there. That's the thing about the next level, God isn't going to be fit into our box. He will move us toward Him, not Himself toward us. He wants us to progress, come up higher, "Let Me show you something you've seen but never seen before."

God completely messes Elijah up, "I'm not confined to the earthquake or the wind or the fire. You'll find Me this time in a still small voice, and next time, who knows?" Then Elijah finds out two important truths: 1) You're not alone in this! There are 7,000 other prophets that are still faithful to the Lord. 2) You can't go to the next level alone. Next level living is about relationships; it's about partnering and connecting.

If you're going to go to new levels in your life you will have to make new connections and build relationships that enable you to move beyond your present place. People are important, they matter to the Lord. God uses people, He creates them with purpose and intention, and so people should matter to us. I am convinced of two things: 1) I should always have a mentor and 2) I should always be a mentor. I live by these principles. There is no way that I can get where I'm going alone. I don't have that ability and don't know all the answers. I need someone in my life that has already gone where I'm going and that person needs to be able to make deposits into my life as well as withdrawals. Mentors have our permission to speak and teach, to impart life and spiritual gifts; they are fathers, friends, and teachers. I also need to be mentoring someone personally, taking what has been deposited into me and depositing it into another. Being mentored and being a mentor takes time and effort. It takes patience and requires risk. The goal is not to create a parrot, but a prophet. It is not one that mimics the other, but one who models what has been mentored, but also discovers who and what they are. Elijah was given the opportunity to mentor Elisha, and in doing so his own life and ministry were enlarged.

There were some requirements for Elisha as he pursued a new level in his life. He quickly learned that if you're going to go somewhere you'll have to leave some things. The first thing that Elisha left was his family and farm; he had to leave the familiar behind. Often we want to enter new dimensions in Christ but don't want to venture far from home. We love the concept of new adventures, but fear the unfamiliar. May I suggest that just because it's new to you doesn't mean it's new to God? He's already gone before us and is waiting there for us. All He asks is that we trust Him. The evidence of our trust and desire for new levels is the effort we make in going after what God has declared can be ours. After Elisha left the familiar, he removed the opportunity to return. The Bible says that he slaughtered his oxen and burned the plowing gear. What Elisha realized is that you cannot afford to leave a rear entry. If we create emergency opportunities that allow us to return to our former lives we will never fully enjoy next level living. It is impossible to go to another level without leaving the last one. He fed the people around him and began his journey with Elijah; the time spent with this mentor would shape his life and ministry.

Elisha received the ministry of impartation in the fullest sense of the word. He saw the man of God in action, was able to learn from him, and to be trained in the ways of God. The Bible doesn't say this, but knowing human nature I'm sure there were moments of impatience and the desire to step out on his own. Each of us face this temptation at some time or another. We want so desperately to be about our Father's business, not realizing that as we serve others faithfully with loyalty we not only learn from them, we also obtain blessings and favor because of our relationship with them.

After many years of serving Elijah there came a moment when it was time for the aged prophet to go be with the Lord. As Elijah prepares to leave he asks Elisha how he could bless and reward him for his service. It was at this moment that Elisha began to ascend to new levels. He would move from aiding the man of God to operating in the same office with a greater anointing of God's power. Life is not a competition with other believers, but a journey through the jungles of humanity, the mastering of the mazes, and the obtaining of new opportunities at new levels.

Here's the challenge of Jesus: unless you leave and forsake your mother and your father, you cannot be my disciple. Next level living involves following the Lord, learning from Him, acting like Him, and receiving His blessing, favor, and power.

Another thing I think is important about going to the next level of our lives is learning to enjoy the journey. Our lives are so busy, so full of essentials and non-essentials, things that we allow to capture our attention and to take our time. Several years ago I was preaching and used an illustration about my love for a certain brand of dress shirts. One of the members of our church was touched by the message and sent me a greeting card a few days later.

Going to the Next Level

Within that card was a check and a note. The note said, "Pastor, here's a check, go out and buy a nice shirt, and while you're at it, don't forget to take the time to smell the roses!" This dear lady realized that it's quite easy to get so busy with life that we miss so much stuff along the way. This is the American way of life - hurry up, we've got places to go, people to meet, and things to see. What happens is that we often fail to really appreciate what we've seen, who we've met, and where we've been. Each level of your life has purpose and meaning. There's a lesson to be learned and people who are divinely deposited into our path. Your journey is incomplete if you don't learn the lessons of the ladder. If you fail to discover that each rung leads you to higher heights and new levels. To learn these lessons you must learn to enjoy the journey.

Next level living is a choice! You are exactly where you want to be, you are doing what you want to do and you have exactly what you want. I can almost hear someone shouting, "Oh no I'm not; this isn't where I want to be!" If you are not progressing, if you are not planning for the future, if you are not seeking opportunities to advance, then you are exactly where you have chosen to be. I may not be exactly at the place I want to be, have all that I desire, or have arrived at my place of assignment or destiny, but if I am progressing, aggressively seeking the place of God's promise, I will arrive in due season, if I don't wear out!

There is another level for your life. It is an exciting place filled with joy and peace, opportunities, and the power to accomplish great things for God. What are you waiting for? Start climbing, new levels await you!

Chapter 12

Become What You Believe!
(Matthews 9:27-31)

When we began this journey together a few chapters back, I told you that you can live life largely. I told you that God can invade the barren places of your life and enlarge your heart so that you can possess everything that He has promised you. We saw in Isaiah's prophecy that out of our emptiness it is possible to give birth to the miraculous…you can live largely in these last days!

We discover the keys to living largely are found as we connect the dots of life. Living largely is about our connections and communication. It's about going through process and taking a journey. Before you can possess great lands you must first become great inwardly. Living largely isn't about a new house or car, but it's about a new you!

This book is about discovering who you are in Christ. It's about receiving a fresh revelation of who He is in you and allowing Him to enlarge your heart, stretching you like a rubber band! As a pastor, I want the people that I pastor to grow and mature. I want them to become big on the inside, to really believe that all things are possible to them. I want them to possess promised lands. It doesn't happen overnight. It takes time and determination, and it requires discipline.

Living largely is about dreaming big and believing that it is possible for us to experience the fulfillment of our dreams. Living largely is about becoming what we believe.

Living Largely

Have you ever read a familiar passage of scripture that all of a sudden became alive to you? I mean, it's like you never saw it this way before. You almost believe that it wasn't there the last time you read your Bible, like God put it in there while you were asleep. That's what happened to me one day while reading Matthew chapter 9. I was reading through the chapter in the Message translation when all of a sudden the words jumped off the page. I think I may have felt like Elizabeth did when Mary told her she was expecting the baby Jesus...I felt something jump inside my belly!

The entire chapter is about God encounters. Jesus has gone here and there touching and changing lives. I love what it says about Jesus when He was crossing over to the other side. I think it tells us that we shouldn't be content to stay where we are. God is inviting us to cross over our hindrances and obstacles so that we can enter new territories in life. As Jesus is crossing over He meets a man whose daughter is dying. He is touched by a woman that has been hemorrhaging for twelve years. He miraculously touches each of these situations on His way to the next encounter.

When He enters the house He has planned to visit, the Bible says there were two blind men following Him. Jesus stops and asks them what they want. They want to see, of course. "Do you believe I can do this?" He asks. "Of course we believe," is their response. Now here's the life changer:

Then become what you believe!

Faith is an action word. It describes what we do with what we are. What we are is more important than what we do, but what we do expresses what we really are. One of the greatest indictments against the Body of Christ is that often our actions don't match our words. We say that we believe that God can do anything, but we act as if He can't. Our foundational truths say that God can still move mountains, but we are paralyzed by mole hills. As believers we live by faith, an invisible realm that has the ability to create and release life and movement. The Bible says that by faith the world was framed (Hebrews 11:3). It also says that without faith we cannot please God (Hebrews 11:6). One writer said that faith is stepping out on nothing and believing until it becomes something. Faith believes that God is who He says He is and that what He says can become a reality in our lives.

    Faith is a language and a lifestyle. People that live and walk by faith have learned to think like God thinks and to speak what His Word declares. The language of faith is not "Christianese." It isn't a religious language known only to church members. Rather, it is the language of the learned, the product of the study of God's Word. Jesus said that there would be issues and mountains in our lives. He told us that we would face impossible obstacles and need miracles in our lives. What He also told us was that every person receives a deposit or a measure of faith, and that our faith grows as we use it. Jesus said that if we speak to a mountain in faith it will move; that if we tell a tree to be plucked up it will be plucked up and cast into the sea. He wasn't saying to go around telling mountains and trees to get out of our way. He was saying that our faith declared by a heart of belief has the ability to change things. If you are going to live largely then you are going to have to expand your vocabulary, to learn how to speak the way God speaks about you. There's something powerful that happens when people begin to talk like God. When they speak His language, it reveals what is truly in their hearts. I'm not suggesting religious speech. By no means am I insinuating that walking around using religious clichés is the language of faith. No, I am suggesting that when you dwell in God and His word is deep within your spirit, your faith life will produce a vocabulary that moves mountains.

Faith is a language, but it's also a lifestyle. The Bible says in three different instances that the just live by faith. It also says that the world and everything that dwells within it were framed by faith. Let me take it one more step; scripture declares that whatever is not of faith is sin! (Romans 14:23). When you receive Jesus into your life He deposits faith into your DNA; it's the ability to see the unseen, hear what no other is hearing, and to believe that the impossible is possible through Christ. We walk and live by faith. This truth is as simple as getting up in the morning. You just get up and believe that your feet and legs will hold you up and allow you to move. As we journey into new places with God we are going by faith, believing that God has spoken to us. We have believed His word to us and are now taking action and moving toward what is yet to be seen with human eyes.

Faith has vision. It sees things that are not there in the natural, but in the Spirit they are coming our way. The reason many people fail to live largely is they have no vision; they only see what is right in front of them. In fact, many only see what everyone else sees. I want to see what no one else can see and to have a personal dream and revelation.

There are some people that refuse to see. They are blinded like Isaiah was in Isaiah 6. The Bible says that in the year that King Uzziah died, Isaiah saw the Lord. Some people never see what God is showing them because they choose to let others stand in their way. We have to remove the obstacles which may mean choosing new friends or changing where we sit in life. What is it in your life that hinders your vision? In the natural some people are born blind or with sight issues, others experience accidents or degenerative diseases that affect their eyesight, while some lose sight with age; others simply refuse to see. The same is true in the spiritual. We are born blind to spiritual things. Jesus came to open our spiritual eyes and open to us a brand new world. Without vision we wander aimlessly through life without direction and inspiration.

The combination of faith and vision allow us to believe God for great things and to see them in our spirit. If we can see it in our spirit, in our inner man, we can become what God has designed our lives to be.

Jesus asked these two blind men a simple and yet profound question: **"Do you really believe that I can do this?"**

I think there are two truths buried within this simple question: 1) Do you believe that I am able to do this? 2) Do you want to change?

The only way God can do anything in a person's life is that they believe that God is not only willing to touch them, but that He can. To live largely one doesn't have to have great knowledge, they have to have confidence in God's ability…faith! Do you believe that God is able to do what you need? Can you see yourself differently than you are right now? Do you believe that God wants to supernaturally intervene in your life?

The other question is, "Do you want to see? Do you really want to change? Many people want things to be different, they just don't want to change? Jesus was asking these two men if they were sure they wanted Him to change their situations, because it would forever change them. True change doesn't happen from the rearranging of outside circumstances, but it takes place from within. Sight isn't based on what is visible outwardly. It is based on what is seen from the inside out. Are you willing to change the direction that you're going? Can you make a total life change? Will you be willing to see differently than you've ever seen?

"Yes, absolutely!" was the quick response of these two blind men, "We want vision. We believe that You can do this." The response of Jesus floors me. In the New King James version, the Bible says, "According to your faith so let it be. And their eyes were opened." But the Message translation says it this way, "He touched their eyes and said, 'Become what you believe.' And it happened. They saw."

What an incredible miracle! Jesus told them to become what they believe they could be. There was no visible proof of change, neither was there any evidence or indication that a healing had taken place. What was there was His touch and their faith. They were being asked to become healed based on their faith in Him….and they did!

Jesus is asking us to do the very same thing. Can we believe God enough to believe and accept what He is promising us? Is it possible to believe in such a way that when we've asked God to do something that we begin to live as if He already has? When we accept Christ into our hearts we believe by faith that He has heard and answered our prayers. Shouldn't we continue that afterward? After all, we're His children and His promise is that He will not withhold any good thing from us (Psalm 84:11). Jesus said, "if we being evil know how to give good things to our children, will not our heavenly Father give the Holy Spirit to them that ask Him?" (Luke 11:13). Have you ever bought something from a friend and asked them to send it to you before you paid them? You ask them to send it and tell them the check is in the mail. There is an act of faith on both sides. On one side you trust them to send it, and on the other side they trust you to mail the check. It's the same with God; He is asking you to trust Him to send what He has promised and you are trusting Him to receive it. Your action reveals your faith, and by faith you take on the essence of what He has promised.

Years ago, the church I was pastoring was in desperate pursuit of revival. We prayed and pleaded for God to move, as we cried out to the Lord for an outpouring of the Holy Spirit in our lives. I preached and taught about revival. It was the all consuming desire of my heart and the subject of my conversation. Regardless of what I was talking about, it always came back to revival. One Sunday I was walking around greeting people when one of our members said to me, "Pastor, you're always talking about having a revival, what if the revival is already here? Maybe the issue is not so much that we need to have a revival, we just need to be a revival! Act on what we've asked God to do and believe it will come to pass!" Looking back, I think what she was saying was: "Become what you believe!"

The objective of this book is about living a life that is larger than the average, normal, everyday, mundane life. It's about expanding our vision and enlarging our territory. It's about becoming big inwardly when everything around us screams that it's time to conserve, reduce, and hide. Living largely isn't something we do, but it's who we become. It's a life change and a mindset. To live largely you have to believe what God says about you and to know who you are in Him. The Word of God has to become alive in

Living Largely

you. It has to be a living word that speaks to you and guides your life. Your eyes have to open and you have to see yourself as God sees you, rather than allowing your vision of God to be filtered by everyday life. When you make the choice to live largely you change the way you think and talk; it affects the way that you live. Your approach to life is unlike those around you that are just surviving. You understand that according to the scripture you have already been made more than a conqueror, that you already have victory, and that in all things you are triumphant. This realization enables you to live your life above the fray, it doesn't prohibit difficulties, but it protects you and helps you to rejoice in spite of the trial.

I know I've already said this - ok, I've said it several times - Living Largely is a Choice! Notice what happened when Jesus told these two blind men to become what they believe: the Bible says, "It happened. They Saw!" When you believe that you can live largely, that Christ has provided better things for you, and that He will take care of you along the way…it will happen!

Becoming what you believe is all about identity change, or maybe it's actually about identity recognition. God created you with the finished product in mind. Over time we take on an identity that is based on environmental and cultural influences; we are the product of our homes, families, churches and friend groups. All of these places and people make deposits into our lives, thus shaping who we become. What has to happen for us to be who God wants us to be is that our lives become redefined by what God speaks into us. I believe that when we receive the word of the Lord into our spirit that we then become responsible, not just for that word, but to become that word. The word of the Lord shapes our life; it creates and recreates our identity as we seek to become what we believe. After we receive the word and determine that it is a defining word, we then begin to wear it as identification tag, doing everything within our power to allow that word to shape and define us. It's kind of like deciding that you want to be a fireman. After the decision is made you begin to train for it. You wear clothing that identifies you as such a person. You learn the language of a fireman and you hang out where firemen are. Believers act like the Bible describes them. You are identified by the Word of God, you connect with other believers, and you hang out where the presence of God is. It's the creation of new life!

Just imagine how different your life could be if you can see yourself as God sees you! How differently would you live if you took the prophetic word seriously and allowed it to shape your life? The Apostle James said that we are to both hear and do the Word. He went on to say that to hear it and not do it is much like looking into a mirror, seeing yourself and then immediately forgetting what you just saw (James 1:22-24). I am responsible for what God says to me and about me. The Word of the Lord is life. There is creative power in the spoken and written Word, but it only works if I wear it on the inside and the outside and become what I believe has been said to and about me!

My youngest daughter wants to be an author. She wants to write books and to illustrate them. She is constantly drawing or writing something. I want to do my best to encourage her, because if she starts this process now she will become what she believes to be her destiny. At this point in life it isn't important if her books are five pages, or if her pictures are hand drawn. What matters is that she has a dream of who and what she believes her identity is and is pursuing her passion. Take a minute right now, close your eyes and look deep into your soul, release your spirit man to dream for just a second...what do you see? Are you looking at where you are presently or are you seeing what can be? Do you have inner insight or do you have blocked vision? Can you see yourself as God has spoken, or is your vision limited to what your present circumstances dictate?

Let's unwrap this a little more. If you can see yourself as God sees you, can you also speak what God is saying to and about you? When children are small and you ask them what they want to be when they grow up, they tell you that they're going to be such and such. They talk about it as if it's just a fact. In their minds there is no question that they will become what they are declaring.

The language of faith we discussed earlier is one that requires that we get it on the inside and release it on the outside. Our words create the image, both in us and for others; they build faith and remove doubts. Words cause life to rise out of what appears to be empty and lifeless.

I can almost hear someone saying, "Well, I've spoken things before and it never happened!" or "That's crazy, just because you say something doesn't mean it's going to happen. I can call my Ford a Mercedes, but it's still a Ford!" The difference is that we are not declaring what we say or think; we're not wildly declaring our own agenda or personal wish list, but we are simply stating what we have heard from God. When God speaks, things happen!

As a pastor, a huge part of my ministry is about receiving a vision or revelation of what the Lord wants me to communicate to our congregation. After I get the vision I have to give the vision. Getting and giving the vision are fairly simple, but getting the people to get it and become it takes time and effort; it doesn't happen overnight. It requires that I keep the vision before them and that I model it, that I wear it before them until they not only see it, but that they believe it can happen in their own lives. Each of us have a unique life vision, something that God has designed for us to become, we need to see that, and we need to discuss it, and then we need to wear it like a badge.

Have you ever seen someone that had something you wanted or was wearing something that appealed to you? Could you see yourself doing that thing or wearing that item? Did you imagine how it would be if you were driving that car or wearing that suit? That's where becoming what you believe begins, but that's only the beginning. You can buy the car and wear the suit, but that doesn't make you the person that you want to be. It takes inner change and the reconstruction of our will. It will require the surrender of your identity and the assuming of something created by God for us. The Apostle Paul said that we are new creations. This means we are being shaped to be just like Jesus.

This thing of becoming doesn't happen overnight, not outwardly. It begins instantly when we submit to Christ and then we begin the lifelong process of conforming to the image of Jesus Christ. To some, this concept might seem to defy the laws of increase and decrease that Jesus spoke of when He said that if any should inherit the Kingdom let them deny themselves and follow Him. But it isn't contrary to the scripture, because in the act of denying ourselves we are stepping out of our box and into His. We commit ourselves to becoming the people that God has always intended for us to be.

The words "it happened" and "they saw" are descriptive of the process of becoming. A baby is born into a family; everything that is necessary for that child to become

Living Largely

an adult is deposited into its body. Outwardly that child is small and developing; it isn't born one day and an adult the next. The child's growth is consistent and gradual, some things developing quicker than others, but everything taking place in its time. Then one day you realize that the little baby you brought home from the hospital is now an adult. They grew up before your very eyes, living in your presence and somehow becoming exactly what they've always meant to be…it happened!

The same is true of each one of us, as we seek to follow Christ, feasting on Him and His Word, taking advantage of every opportunity to pursue His purpose and grow in His grace. One day we're newborn babies in Christ struggling to survive and overcome the obstacles of life, living faithfully according to His promises, and the next thing you know, you have become a man or a woman of God that is living and walking victoriously!

As a new believer, I daydreamed of big things in God. I read the New Testament and saw word pictures of men and women of God living exciting lives in Jesus. They weren't problem free lives or lives always filled with material prosperity, but they were lives that radiated the belief that if you follow God and love Him with all of your heart, He will take care of you and you can live a powerful life. I wanted to be like those men and women I read about…and I still do!

It is possible to live largely in these last days. It is possible to live victoriously and to experience the fullness of God's blessings in your life. It is possible to overcome the obstacles and to seize the opportunities that present themselves to us. It is possible to come to the end, to experience all that the end times present us, and enjoy an abundant entrance into the Kingdom of God.

Become What You Believe!

The choice is ours…the choice is yours…the choice is mine!

I'm living largely…what about you?

Conclusion

Throughout the pages of this book I have attempted to describe a life that reaches beyond the everyday "let's get by" mentality that so many people have accepted as the norm. It is my firm conviction that even in difficult times children of God excel and live largely. I'm not suggesting that we don't struggle or experience setbacks. I am boldly declaring that it is God's will for us to live differently than everyone else!

One day as I was thinking on the things of the Lord I heard the Holy Spirit speak into my spirit a very simple word. He said, "Move beyond Normal." You can imagine my next thought, "I'm hearing things or I've gone crazy!" Immediately my mind was drawn to a story in the Book of Mark where four men brought their paralyzed friend to Jesus for healing. There was such a crowd that they couldn't enter the house. Most of us would have returned home and complained about the crowd, the wasted trip and the cost of travel. Not these guys. Rather than going home, they ripped the roof off of the house and lowered their friend down into the presence of Jesus. Their friend received his healing because his friends were willing to move beyond normal.

Normal is a standard set by one for another to live by. God's normal and our normal are quite different. Our normal allows us to live small-minded lives, to settle for less than what God intends for us. God's normal challenges us to live largely and to stretch as far as we can; so that when we snap, we find ourselves soaring into new dimensions of life!

Citations

1. Pastor Michael Sloan, Senior Pastor of Oasis World Outreach, 35636 Highway 54 West, Zephyrhills, FL 33541

2. Pastor Michael Sloan, Senior Pastor of Oasis World Outreach, 35636 Highway 54 West, Zephyrhills, FL 33541

3. The Shack, p. 175, William P. Young, Windblown Media, 4680 Calle Norte, Newbury Park, CA 91320

4. Pastor Ernest E. Brown. Pastor of the Christian Center, The Christian Center, 9105 AL Highway 69, Arab, AL 35016

5. Soulprint, Mark Batterson, pastor of National Community Church, 205 F Street NE, Washington DC, 20002

6. The Present, C. Spencer Johnson, Crown Publishing Group, 1745 Broadway, New York, NY 10019

7. John Maxwell
http://www.thomasnelson.com/consumer/product_detail.asp?sku=0785272674&title=Living_at_the_Next_Level

8. Next Level Living, p. 1, Pastor Rich Rogers, Charisma House, 600 Rinehart Rd, Lake Mary, FL 32746

About the Author

Neil P. Smith began preaching at the age of 16. His ministry began as an evangelist, taking him throughout the United States. He has also served as a pastor and associate pastor since 1989. His ministry is one of evangelistic fervor with a prophetic nature and a pastor's heart. His humor and wit cause people to be encouraged. The revelation and insight of the heart draw them into God's presence. Neil's commitment to the scripture allows his preaching and teaching to speak to people a present truth. Neil has traveled extensively throughout the US as well as missions trips to Haiti and Kenya. He is the director of Neil Smith Ministries.

To schedule Neil you may contact him at:

www.nsmithministries.org

neil@nsmithministries.org

Kingdom Kaught Publishing
Denton Maryland USA
www.kingdomkaughtpublishing.com

www.ingramcontent.com/pod-product-compliance
Lightning Source LLC
Chambersburg PA
CBHW031255290426
44109CB00012B/585